WHAT'S HAPPENING

Making Sense of 2012
and a
World in Chaos

Wesley Ewell

Quercus Publishing
Cape Cod, Massachusetts

Copyright © 2011 Wesley Ewell
All rights reserved.
No part of this publication may be reproduced,
stored in a retrieval system,
or transmitted in any form
or by any means, electronic, mechanical,
photocopying, recording or otherwise,
without the prior written permission
of the publisher.

ISBN: 978-0-9827470-4-9

Published by Quercus Publishing
Cape Cod, Massachusetts
www.quercuspublishing.com

Cover photo of hurricane Katrina
hitting the Gulf coast courtesy of NASA

"We must be willing
to get rid of the life we planned,
so as to have the life
that is waiting for us."

Joseph Campbell

ACKNOWLEDGEMENTS

Writing may be a lonely task, but it is not done alone. I wish to thank all those who helped me in this effort, especially the following people: my daughters for their patience reviewing countless drafts and gently suggesting ways to improve my message; the gifted psychic April Sheerin, who told me to "write your book;" astrologer Arlan Wise, who directed me to the works of two of her teachers for a rational analysis of this ancient art; and Philosopher and Professor Emeritus Eugene Bammel, who lent me more than a few words of wisdom. Thanks also to my friends in the Cape Cod Writers Center for their critiques and encouragement.

CONTENTS

INTRODUCTION 1
   An overview of what this book is all about.

PART I – A SPIRITAL AWAKENING 9
   A narrative of the author's introduction to non-religious spirituality, with descriptions of some basic concepts of metaphysics.

PART II – WHAT'S HAPPENING 52
   A summary of many of the changes we are seeing in our world and our personal lives.

PART III – WE HAVE BEEN WARNED 105
   Some of the key sources that have foretold the current changes in our world.

PART IV – WHAT TO EXPECT 149
   An introduction to a different world from what we have known.

PART V – WHAT THIS MEANS TO US 202
   How the new planetary energy might affect us individually.

EPILOGUE 233
   Background on how this book came to be.

NOTES AND REFERENCES 238
   Where to look for more information.

To Connie Doyle
who taught me to write

INTRODUCTION

Our world is not about to end. Despite the claims of the fearful; despite the ancient prophecies; and despite the chaos seen in every corner of our lives, the earth will continue to turn and most of us will still be here after December 21, 2012.

Our world is changing, though. When the current chaos settles down we will all find ourselves living in a very different environment from anything we have known before. Our politics and governments; our financial situations; our weather and climate; the way we work; and every aspect of our personal lives will have changed.

After a lifetime of observation and study I believe I have discovered a rational explanation for what's happening in our world at this confusing time. I have also developed a logical and common sense understanding of the nature of our universe and our purpose in this experience we call life.

This book is my offering of a different way of thinking about how we have been living and how the changes we are seeing in our world represent a positive new way of thinking and behaving. I ask you to keep an open mind while reading it, and to consider that there may be some new truths in what I have written.

WHAT'S HAPPENING

If you open any book with the date 2012 or the word apocalypse in the title, you might think we are all about to become toast. Many of these books convey terrifying messages of imminent doom and prophesy of global calamity. Television shows and movies feed our fears of extraterrestrial invasions, government conspiracies, and hidden dangers.

An Internet search will reveal even more frightening information, with references to the Hopi Map, the Mayan calendar, the biblical Book of Revelation, and predictions made by the medieval doctor and astronomer, Nostradamus. These ancient prophecies have often been interpreted to predict a cataclysmic end to our earth and all living things on it around the turn of the millennium or, more specifically, on December 21, 2012.

Some predict the end will come in a nuclear holocaust that will wipe us all out. Others say we will be hit by an unprecedented worldwide earthquake, or by an asteroid that will shroud the world in darkness or knock the planet out of its orbit. Scientists tell us that asteroid collisions have happened many times in the past—one of these events was most likely responsible for killing all the dinosaurs some sixty-five million years ago.

Our world may have come perilously close to nuclear annihilation when political tensions between the Soviet Union and the United States rose to dangerous levels between the end of World War II and the collapse of the Soviet Union in 1991. Both countries had enough nuclear bombs to destroy all life on earth. The resulting tensions became so critical that Great Britain adopted a "Doomsday Plan" for the seemingly inevitable Armageddon.[1]

Dig a little deeper, though, and read the works of experts in Mayan studies, biblical history, and medieval spirituality, and you will find a positive interpretation of the old prophesies. Specialists in Mesoamerican studies, such as Daniel Pinchbeck and John Major Jenkins, claim the Mayan calendar foretells not the end of the world, but the coming of a golden age of peace and prosperity.[2]

Biblical historians, including Professor Bart D. Ehrman of the University of North Carolina at Chapel Hill, tell us the Book of Revelation of John is not a prediction of Armageddon, but an example of a popular literary form of its time—a precursor of our modern science fiction—that described a fanciful and imminent end to the world.[3]

Nostradamus saw widespread destruction from what he described as "a rain of fire from the sky." That could be interpreted as either a nuclear war or an asteroid. But he also prophesized, in a letter to his son Cesar, that the earth would then enter a Golden Age, and his prophesies for human life on the planet continued until the year 3797.[4]

WHAT'S HAPPENING

The doomsday scenarios may have been misinterpreted, or they may have been correct but are no longer valid because something changed. I believe we are now experiencing a fundamental shift in planetary energy that is changing the way we think, the way we act, and the way we live our lives. We are seeing chaos and destruction all over the planet, but nothing so dire that it suggests the end of our world.

This may not be Armageddon but it might be the apocalypse. Armageddon is the violent end to all life on earth. But the word *apocalypse* is derived from the Greek word *ápokálypsis,* which literally means revelation of that which is hidden. Metaphysicists tell us the apocalypse is not the end of the world but a time when the barrier—or veil—between our physical world and the spirit world is eased, allowing us more direct access to spiritual knowledge, personal enlightenment, and unusual abilities that have been hidden from us until now.

There can be no question our world is changing in ways we have not seen before. And the changes that we hear about daily can be frightening and confusing. Our weather seems to have gone crazy. Earthquakes, volcanic eruptions, tornados, floods, hurricanes, firestorms, and other natural calamities appear to be overwhelming us.

Governments and national boundaries are shifting. Political affiliations and policies are moving in new directions. Hubris, greed, and mismanagement are crippling businesses and economic institutions that were thought to be unshakable. Secrets and unethical behavior are being exposed as never before, not only bringing down leaders in business, government, and religion, but also affecting our individual lives and personal relationships.

Our churches are struggling to remain relevant as their adherents seek more direct and meaningful spiritual nourishment. Traditional views of marriage and other relationships are being questioned as never before. Individuals and institutions that dominate or control the behavior and thinking of others are meeting with rebellion, rejection, and disobedience—or simply being ignored—especially by the younger generation now becoming adults.

Women are moving into positions of authority and changing the way businesses and governments are managed. People of all ages are shedding the roles and images that others have imposed upon them.

We are beginning to see through the lies and misrepresentations of our political and religious leaders. The young people now emerging into adulthood are quietly living by a different set of ethics, more concerned with issues of social justice and personal fulfillment than with acquisition of material things and any concern about the behavior of others. They seem to be more secure and confident in themselves and their lives than their parents and grandparents were at that age, even as jobs and social safety nets are being threatened.

What's happening may not be the end of the world as predicted, but the end of the world as we have known it. This may not be the end of civilization, but the beginning of an entirely new world-wide culture. We appear to be in the midst of a breakdown of old systems that no longer work for us. I think we are also seeing the introduction of new ways of thinking and acting that supplant fear with compassion, secrecy with transparency, and war with peaceful cooperation.

The apparently chaotic breakdown of both our physical environment and our social institutions may not be random events. And the sudden collapse of so many political and business systems seems to be more than mere coincidence. All of these events appear to be related—closely connected to each other—and necessary for us to adapt to an evolving new world energy.

The old systems must fail by their own fault before the new systems can replace them. This shift in thinking and behavior is not going to happen suddenly on a given day or within a given year. These changes began three hundred years ago and it could be many more decades before they are fully realized. Within the last few years, though, we have seen a rapid acceleration of the movement toward this new order, as a majority of the world's population becomes more enlightened and begins to think and act in new ways.

Strangely, we have been told this would happen. For more than forty years we have been receiving information from unknown sources that has foretold the current weather patterns, the political upheavals, and many of the news events that surprise us daily. These messages have come to us through ordinary people who never thought of themselves as psychics or seers.

Some people think this information is encoded in our genes, or coming from extraterrestrial beings. Or might it be coming from a spirit world that we cannot normally see, hear, feel, or touch? An increasing number of people around the globe believe this is so. Some, including many of our children and grandchildren, seem to be intrinsically aware of this deeper world of spirit, and far more connected to it than are their elders. We all accept the ancient scriptures that were delivered to the world by revelation to individuals. These new revelations might be coming to us in the same way from the same source.

Perhaps the time has come for our society to release its hold on the purely scientific notion known as logical positivism, with its demand that we accept only that which we can measure and prove to exist. Nearly all of us worship some form of god that we cannot see, touch, measure, or define.

We simply accept this belief on faith alone. Why shouldn't we also accept that there is more to our reality than that which is clearly visible? Maybe we need to open our minds and find new ways to measure and define this experience we call life.

Our earth may not be headed to destruction, but it and we appear to be going through a massive and fundamental change. Many of the old rules and the old ways of thinking and acting that have dominated our lives for millennia must be discarded. When things settle down, our physical world, our societal values, and our personal lives could be very different from what we have known.

We may also find we have gained new personal insights and abilities that give us much more power to shape our individual lives and create the reality that we most desire. This is a time to challenge attitudes and beliefs that no longer work. It is also a time for celebration as we welcome a global movement toward a more peaceful, spiritual, and enlightened planet.

PART I – A SPIRITUAL AWAKENING

<u>Transcendental Memories</u>

The Town of Concord, Massachusetts, evokes visions of Paul Revere and the Minutemen; a band of ragtag militants defeating the highly organized British army. Concord has an equally rich history as the birthplace of modern American literature, and of the kind of progressive social and spiritual thinking that is only now beginning to re-emerge in our society. In the nineteenth century it was the home of Ralph Waldo Emerson, Henry David Thoreau, Bronson Alcott and his daughter Louisa May, and other literary giants who enjoyed the company of peers in this village a few miles west of Boston.

On a frigid January day in Concord nearly thirty years ago, my mind was not on literary giants—I just wanted to get warm. Despite the wind and snow and bitter cold, my friend Joan and I were touring the historic sites with Joan's sister Carol and Carol's husband, Phil. Carol and Phil had come east for a visit from their home in the Rocky Mountains. Phil was a college mathematics professor and, like many academics, was deeply curious about all aspects of life. He struck me as more of a philosopher than a scientist.

After a brief tour of historic sites, and a quick walk across the Old North Bridge and up the path to the Minuteman statue, we welcomed the warmth of the Colonial Inn. We quickly settled in around the fireplace in the bar room. This modest building at the north end of the Concord town green had become a popular restaurant and inn, known for its traditional New England food and colonial era furnishings. It serves the best Indian pudding you will find anywhere. The inn had originally been Emerson's home, and Thoreau had lived there for a while too.

Ralph Waldo Emerson began his career as an ordained minister in the Unitarian Church. As he developed his idealist philosophy, however, he found even the relatively liberal Unitarian church to be too rigid. At a time when the Christian Bible was widely believed to be literal truth, Emerson saw it as figurative allegory. He was an early advocate of living spiritually without adhering to traditional doctrine and religious rituals.

Henry David Thoreau was highly intelligent, underappreciated, and considered more than a little odd in his own time. He rebelled against authority and conformity, had trouble with existing political and social systems that he considered to be broken, and had a burning desire to change and improve the world. Thoreau clearly stepped to the music of a different drummer.[5]

We were the only people in the bar—the dinner crowd would not arrive for a few more hours. As we thawed our fingers around mugs of hot Jamaican coffee, we talked about how Emerson and Thoreau might have sat in front of that same fireplace with their friends Bronson Alcott, Nathaniel Hawthorne, and a promising young poet visiting from New York named Walt Whitman.

We might have been sitting in the same spot where these creative minds envisioned an ideal world. A world where education was free and available to everyone, where women were equal to men in every way, where children were taught to think independently, religions sought truth instead of preaching dogma, and governments served all of their constituents, not just the rich and powerful.

These men, and a group of their contemporaries in Boston area literary circles, came to be known as the Transcendentalists, although Emerson never liked that name. The Transcendentalists originated the concepts of universal public education and of child-centered schooling that recognizes the ability of children to develop their own ideas. At that time, educational opportunities were relatively limited for all but the most privileged children, and teaching focused primarily on instilling obedience and rote memorization of facts.

Bronson Alcott tried to form a utopian community of Transcendentalists on his farm, which he ironically called Fruitlands. His experiment failed, though, partly due to the harsh New England weather, but largely because Alcott's idealistic ideas proved to be economically unrealistic.[6]

Although the transcendental movement never carried far beyond its New England roots, the ideas that arose from its published works transformed many aspects of our society in ways that are still felt today.

A New Worldview

Maybe Emerson's ghost had joined our fireside musings, or it might have been the Jamaican coffees taking effect, but our conversation at the inn eventually turned to thoughts of the nature of life and reality. Joan insisted she was a rationalist, convinced by hard life lessons that this world and everything in it was nothing more than a random occurrence. She believed that all aspects of our existence simply end when our bodies die.

Phil disagreed, suggesting instead that the life we are experiencing is only a small part of an infinite existence that is following some grand plan. He explained that we actually have complete freedom of choice and control of our individual lives. He claimed that we are constantly choosing every detail of our existence from an infinite variety of potential realities.

I had long thought that there must be more to our existence than that which we can see, hear, touch, and measure. There were simply too many aspects of life that seemed to be beyond explanation. I also sensed that throughout my life, figurative doors had been opened for me—and others closed—by some force that I could not identify.

I believed in God, although I had come to realize that the image of God that I had been taught as a child was clearly irrational. I knew that God was not some judgmental father figure that rewarded those who followed church dogma and punished those who disobeyed. So Phil's statements piqued my interest and I wanted to know more. Might there actually be guardian angels or greater aspects of our own personas that exist outside of our physical bodies?

Phil went on to explain that he had been reading a series of unusual books by the poet and author, Jane Roberts. He said that these books were transcripts that Roberts had dictated while in a trance state. Her trance pronouncements were recorded in detail, complete with annotations about the weather and the behavior of their pets, by her husband, Robert Butts. Roberts attributed the source of this information to a spiritual entity known only as Seth. Seth did not claim to be a god or a saint. He said he had lived many lives on earth as a human, the most recent being that of an Italian who immigrated to the United States.

When I expressed interest in learning more, Phil suggested I start with the second book in the series, which is titled *Seth Speaks*. He said to then go back and read the first book, titled *The Seth Material*. *Seth Speaks* was dictated by Seth, while *The Seth Material* chronicles Jane Roberts' earliest experience with trance channeling and the events leading to the production of these books.

The next day I bought those two books, and the third of the series, titled *The Nature of Personal Reality*. In this book, Seth explains how each of us creates our individual reality by our thoughts, and how all of us together create our common reality. There were other Seth books on the shelf, but I would get to them later. I proceeded to devour this material. It answered so many questions I had been asking for years—and so many more that I had not thought to ask.

The Seth books seemed to present a rational explanation of who we are, where we come from, and why we are here. Over the next few years I read them all, frequently visiting my favorite bookstores in hopes of finding a new one. These books are not easy to read. Grammatical structures are often awkward, and Robert Butts' annotations can be distracting. Every sentence tends to be so loaded with meaning, and so begging thoughtful interpretation, that the reader is frequently forced to stop and think about the statements they make.

The magnitude of the concepts and explanations presented by Seth is almost beyond comprehension. His basic messages are that we are each far more than our mortal selves; that we are all part of a universal energy source; and that our thoughts create our material world and our lives within it.

Seth confirms the existence of God, referring to God as *All That Is*. He says that God cannot be defined in our terms, but suggests that we might think of God as a form of pure energy. Seth also confirms the existence of a vast spirit world of angels and guides that is deeply involved with our lives, but which most of us have not been able to sense because this knowledge would confuse us.

Seth says that the essence of whom we are—which we call our souls—live forever. He further says that only a small portion of our souls occupy our bodies, and that we are in constant communication with our greater selves through our intuition and dreams. Seth says that we are much more than our physical bodies, and that when our bodies die, we retain ethereal bodies that are just as real to us, but far less restricted in what they can do.

Seth confirms that we reincarnate multiple times into this earthly existence so that we might fully experience the nature of physical being. He says that time has no reality except to allow us to make sense of this particular existence. As a consequence, our past and future lives effectively happen all at once. In other words, we not only come this way more than once, we come this way more than once at the same time.

Seth's pronouncements, as strange and comprehensive as they are, make a lot of sense to me. They are also consistent with other sources that have written of the nature of reality, including the original teachings of Jesus Christ, Mohammed, the Buddha, and the other prophets who inspired all of our world's major religions.

The idea that we bring into this world knowledge and experience from other lives—both past and future—as well as bits of the wisdom of the ages from the spirit world, makes ultimate sense. I have always thought it unlikely that our individual personalities and talents, in all of their complexity, could possibly result solely from childhood experience and training. It seems far more obvious to me that we arrive into this world with a lot of software preinstalled.

Jane Roberts authored at least twenty-five books, eight of which were dictated by Seth. The difference in literary quality and depth of thought between the books she wrote and those she dictated in trance are so stark and notable as to convince even the most skeptical reader that they did not come from the same source.

All of Roberts' books remain in print today. Her students and followers have published additional books of their experiences with her, and continue to promote the Seth material through lectures, seminars, on-line forums, videos, and recordings.[7]

The Seth books are notable in that they mark the beginning of a new round of apparent communication from the spirit world that reached a mass audience. They convey positive visions of a changed future, as well as logical explanations of past events and the nature of personal reality.

One of Seth's pronouncements is that each of us influences the thinking and behavior of every person we encounter in some important way. We come into someone's life for a reason, and leave it when that reason no longer exists. Clearly Phil appeared in my life to introduce me to Seth. I do know that I influenced Joan's life, and that she profoundly influenced mine. Joan and I eventually chose to follow separate paths, however, and I never saw Phil again after that day in Concord.

An Authentic Psychic

Brenda did not look like a psychic. Slender, attractive, and apparently shy, this 30-something homemaker and mother of five daughters simply did not fit my image of a seer. I pictured a psychic as a pudgy older woman dressed like a gypsy and reading a crystal ball.

I also did not believe there was such a thing as a person who could actually see energy fields, divine the future, and sense the thoughts of those around her. Brenda's husband Dan and I worked together, and the three of us, along with our secretary, Natasha, were in Atlanta for a convention not long after that frigid January day in Concord.

We were chatting over dinner one evening when Dan announced that his wife was a witch. Nat and I laughed nervously, assuming he was attacking Brenda's attitude and that we were about to get more information about their relationship than we wanted to hear. Dan assured us that he was serious and that Brenda had abilities that most of us could not understand.

Brenda then admitted that she was able to foresee events that were about to happen to people around her. She emphasized, though, that the events she saw were only possible realities, and that any of them could be changed by conscious thought. She said she avoided being with large groups of people because she would become overwhelmed with messages about everyone in the room.

Our conversation had suddenly become much more animated. Brenda told us how she received communications from the spirit world, whether she wanted to or not, and how she learned to develop her talents with help from her grandmother, who also had these abilities. When she began to describe the nature of reality and how we fit into it, I realized she was saying exactly what Seth had said. I asked if she knew of the Seth books and she said she did not. At this point my skepticism began to fade.

Whenever I have heard new information, whether it is scientific, political, spiritual, or otherwise, I have always tested it in my mind against my knowledge of the world as I have experienced it. I ask "Does this make sense?" when deciding whether to accept or reject the information. I had recently added a second test: "Does this information come from more than one source?" Here was dramatic new information coming from a second source.

Dan then told us that Brenda also reads tarot cards. Once again, he was pushing the limits of my credulity. I thought of tarot cards as theatrical props that sideshow fortunetellers use to distract people they were conning while they stalled for time. But Brenda had shown herself to be too authentic to question, so I agreed when she offered to do a reading in the privacy of my hotel room.

First Brenda shuffled the cards, and then she asked me to cut them into three stacks. She laid the cards out on the table face down in a particular pattern before turning them over one at a time. With each card, Brenda made an observation related to some aspect of my life. She also seemed to move deeper into my psyche with each observation. It soon became clear that she was sensing far more specific information about my personal life and thoughts than I had ever shared with Dan or with anybody else.

Brenda knew that I was divorced, but neither she nor Dan had ever met my ex-wife. Nevertheless, she not only knew details of my ex's personality, but she also knew of the motivating forces behind her behavior. How, I asked, could a deck of picture cards give her such insight?

Brenda explained that the cards only served as catalysts for her psychic abilities. She was not sure how they worked. She only knew that the various characters and symbols on the cards would trigger thoughts or feelings in her mind. She also admitted that she did not express all the images she saw, lest she unnecessarily frighten or sadden the people for whom she was reading the cards.

Over the next two years, Brenda read cards for me several more times. Each time she offered valuable insight and guidance as I struggled to deal with the aftermath of my divorce and many other aspects of midlife changes. The last time she read for me she also talked about two other metaphysical concepts that meant nothing to me at the time but which became important later. One was energy auras and the other was soul lives. Seth had mentioned both and I figured these were just more ideas that were important to psychics but did not affect my life.

As usual, Brenda was late for one of our readings—this time about twenty minutes late. The first thing she said, though, was "Oh good. I'm glad you're not upset." How did she know that? Brenda explained that all living beings, including animals and plants, have an aura—a colorful energy field that emanates from our bodies. She said most people cannot see these auras, but that she sees them around everybody. She said my aura is normally bluish-green, but if I had been angry or upset my aura would have shown bands of orange.

Later in the reading, Brenda told me that a "baby soul" in a position of power where I worked wanted to get rid of me. Being more concerned about my job, I did not ask what she meant by the term baby soul. I later learned it is a person who has lived fewer lives on earth and has not attained the level of wisdom and spiritual enlightenment that is seen in an older soul. A few weeks later my position was eliminated and I found myself unemployed.

I left the company with a severance package that included use of a field office located at the intersection of two busy highways just outside of Boston. Every workday I would commute to the field office and make a full-time job of looking for a position. Late one night during this time Brenda called me.

She apologized for calling so late, but said she had just had a vivid image that associated me with an automobile accident in which a petite woman is killed or severely injured. She sensed that I would not be hurt, and might not be directly involved in the accident, but that it could be a close encounter. She said she saw a highway overpass with large signs mounted to it—which is not as common in Massachusetts as it is in some other states—but that she could not discern any other details.

The next day, as I was leaving the field office, I saw ahead of me a highway overpass with two large signs on it. Just before I got to the overpass, a small car coming from the other direction jumped the median, crossed the road right in front of me, and went up the embankment to my right. The rush hour traffic was heavy but moving quickly and I was past the scene and up the ramp before it sunk in what happened. I did not stop, as it would have been dangerous, so I have no idea if the driver was a petite woman or was hurt. If there had ever been any doubt in my mind about Brenda's psychic abilities, though, it was gone now.

A Different Astrology

At some point Brenda suggested that I have my astrological chart prepared, and introduced me to an astrologer whom she admired. Again, my preconceptions intruded. Like most people, I had been amused by the astrology columns in newspapers and magazines, but did not take them seriously.

These daily predictions are simply too general to have any real meaning. How could the position of the sun on the day of my birth have anything at all to do with my activities today, forty years later? Because of my regard for Brenda's abilities and advice, however, I agreed to meet with the astrologer.

David did not seem like a wizard or a fraud. A quiet and introspective man in his early forties, his day job was as an elementary grade teacher in a small private school. His apartment looked like a used book store and his manner was that of a serious academic. David explained that astrology is an ancient science that dates to before the first recorded history. He said that serious astrologers go beyond the popular features found in the newspapers.

David told me that astrologers calculate the positions of the sun, planets, and other objects in our solar system, relative to each other and to their positions in our galaxy. They then predict the effects of the position and movement of each heavenly body on our thinking and behavior based upon eons of experience in correlating human behavior to celestial activity. He told me that these celestial movements are constantly changing and influence both individual and group behavior.

David had plotted my chart before I arrived for this first session. This involved calculating the positions and movement of the sun, moon, and other heavenly bodies, relative to the exact time and location of my birth. He then was able to judge how and to what extent each of those celestial objects had affected my life to date and how they would influence it in the future.

I found David's analysis to be startlingly on the mark for my past experience, and therefore credible for his future predictions. He spoke of my artistic bent and my discomfort with conventional beliefs and systems. He told me I was a teacher and had wisdom that I should share with others. Whatever the source of his knowledge, there was obviously something to it and I returned for a second reading a few months later.

I might have continued with regular visits, but not long after my second session with him, Brenda called informing me that David had died. His death was apparently quick and unexpected, resulting from massive internal hemorrhaging.

As a society, we have come to expect sudden death from heart attacks and traffic accidents. We accept the apparent inevitability of slow death from various forms of cancer. But we do not expect a relatively young and otherwise healthy individual to simply drop dead without warning. Seth said we each choose when and where to be born and when and how to die. Maybe David found he was needed somewhere else.

I have since learned that astrology has been around longer than any religion. The knowledge of astrology may have been given to human society at its creation. Nicholas Campion, a respected British expert in this field, documents evidence of astrological study to before the earliest days of recorded history in his book *The Dawn of Astrology*.[8] Professor Campion notes that astrology is practiced in various forms by all cultures throughout the world. It remains an important element today in the culture of India, and was widely practiced throughout Europe until denounced by church leaders in the seventeenth century.

Scientists and scholars typically dismiss astrology as a frivolous diversion. If instead they studied it with respect, they might find clues to more efficient ways to solve some of our society's most vexing problems. Astrology tells us that there are times when communications thrive and times when everything is confused and misunderstood. It suggests that, as described in the Book of Ecclesiastes, there is a time for every activity under heaven.[9]

I suspect that those of us who follow this practice tend to have fewer frustrations with life's daily struggles than do those who continue to push and fight against every obstacle. The fact that astrology has lasted throughout human history demands that we keep trying to learn more about it. Maybe those scientists who tried to test astrology used the wrong measurements or failed to ask the right questions.

Multiple Lives

A.J. and I lived and worked together for several years in the late 1980s. If there is such a thing as soul mates, we are a pair. We could pass for brother and sister, with the same complexion and the same hair color and texture. We are blessed with similar intellectual abilities and artistic talents. We share the same rare blood type.

One of my daughters once noted, after seeing us relaxing on the deck with our feet on the rail, that we even have feet that look alike. Seth says that soul mates are fragments of the same spiritual entity. A.J. had read the Seth books and was as curious about the spiritual life as I.

There is an unseen downside to being soul mates, though. While it can be fun to share your life with someone who thinks and acts as you do, A.J. and I learned that it can also lead to problems. To paraphrase the nursery rhyme of the girl with the curl on her forehead, when two people who are so alike are good, they are very, very good; but when they are bad, they can be horrid.

A.J. and I eventually parted ways and she moved to the West Coast, but we remain friends. She has since earned a doctoral degree in spiritual theology, and writes and lectures widely on the nature of reality. One day, not long after we split up, A.J. called and excitedly told me about a new series of books she had discovered. She said they were similar to the Seth books in that they were dictated by a spiritual entity. This spirit was known as Michael and communicated through a group of channelers in the San Francisco Bay area.

I immediately went out and bought a copy of *The Michael Handbook*, by Jose Stevens and Simon Warwick-Smith.[10] Once again, I was fascinated by new information that explained so much of that which had long been confusing to me. Just as Seth's *The Nature of Personal Reality* explains how our reality works, *The Michael Handbook* explains how our inner personalities are formed and defined. Unlike the hard to read Seth books, however, this one is direct and straightforward in its descriptions of the nature of our personalities.

In this book, Michael describes in detail the various aspects of our physical, intellectual, and motivational characteristics. He also explains how all these characteristics change as we journey through many lifetimes toward spiritual enlightenment—complete understanding of the nature of life and reality. These include detailed descriptions of soul ages and how they influence world affairs; soul levels, which represent steps in our spiritual growth; roles, modes, goals, and attitudes that we assume; chief features, body types, and centering. There is also an appendix on the coming planetary shift, which is the primary subject of this book and which we will explore further in later chapters.

While the Seth books were dictated by a single spiritual entity through a single channeler, the Michael material was dictated from a group of spiritual entities collectively called Michael through a group of channelers working together. More than 1600 pages of transcripts from these channelings were destroyed in the Oakland Hills firestorm of 1991, but enough material was salvaged to produce at least sixteen books by several of the people involved.

Two of the most useful to me are *The World According to Michael* and *Upcoming Changes: The Next 20 years*, both authored by Joya Pope. Another member of this group, Chelsea Quinn Yarborough, wrote four books: *Messages from Michael, More Messages from Michael, Michael's People,* and *Michael for the Millennium.* This last book—along with Pope's *Upcoming Changes*—was written nearly two decades ago, but outlined many of the world events that we are experiencing now.

The Michael material is thoroughly consistent with the Seth material. Both describe God as an energy entity and use the term *All That Is*. Both say that we are each and all fragments of this energy and that our existence is far greater than our physical experience on earth. Both confirm that our basic essence—our souls—live forever and are following a path toward enlightenment, or knowledge of who we are and where we came from. While it is possible—or even likely—that the Michael channelers had been influenced by the Seth books, their affirmation of these concepts reinforces Seth's credibility with additional information.

This description of following a path to enlightenment is also the basic teaching of all major religions, but some church leaders seem to have either missed the point or misinterpreted the message. It says that we are all working toward a deeply understood knowledge of reality and our place in it, as well as a return to our understanding of our relationship to God.

Japanese Buddhism calls this state of understanding *satori*. Chinese and Indian Buddhism and Hinduism call it *nirvana*. This state of understanding may have been what Christ meant when he said we must be born again in order to enter the kingdom of heaven.[11]

Recognizing that we are all on a path to enlightenment will help us to better understand the changes that are happening in our world today. As we move along this path, we mature in our thinking and our behavior, becoming wiser and godlier at each step along the way. We also become serene and begin to feel that our lives are more personally fulfilling.

Spiritual Growth

Nearly all of the world's religions teach that we go somewhere else when we die.[12] Some say we go to heaven where our worldly cares vanish and we enjoy an eternity of bliss. Some threaten that if we do not behave in a morally superior way, we go to hell, where we will suffer for all eternity.

When logic intrudes, it tells us that both of these scenarios are absurd in their simplicity. This concept of heaven sounds eternally boring, with no challenges or lessons and no opportunity for growth. And this concept of hell flies in the face of the universal religious teachings of repentance, atonement, and redemption.

Both Seth and Michael tell us that life after death is not very different from life on earth. They say we continue to grow emotionally, interact with family members and friends, hone our talents, and make plans for the future. The only difference is that we are no longer burdened after death by our physical bodies, the constraints of time, or any forces of evil. Most importantly, they teach that we keep coming back to earth in order to experience this physical life and its many challenges.

This concept of reincarnation teaches that each of us is born into this world hundreds of times in order to experience all aspects of physical life. Through these experiences we gradually become more enlightened and more aware of the nature of reality and of our spiritual heritage. Support for this idea can be found in the original texts and teachings of all the world's major religions. It is also found in the channeled texts cited here.

While the concept of reincarnation is not currently embraced by the major Western religions—and is actively denied by evangelicals—it was apparently included in their scriptures until excised by the Roman emperor Constantine the Great in A.D. 325, an action that was confirmed by the Second Council of Constantinople meeting in A.D. 553.[13] It remains an important aspect of Eastern religions, and is universally accepted by psychic mediums, spiritualists, and Metaphysicists.

Our culture acknowledges that each of us is born with unique talents, abilities, and attitudes that make us different from all others in measurable ways. We know, for instance, that some people are more athletic than others. We see that some are more creative, whether it is in art, music, writing, technology, or invention. We acknowledge that some are smarter, or show more emotional maturity, than their peers. These measurements play important roles in determining our career paths, personal interests, and positions in society.

We have not recognized, however, that some people are more enlightened than others—wiser and further along on the path to more godly attitudes and behavior. Yet a consideration of this attribute of human behavior opens a window of understanding that throws new light on many of the problems we are dealing with every day in world politics, local government, and personal relationships. It also illuminates the path that every one of us is following as we move through our daily lives.

Philosophers and psychologists have often explored the idea that there are measurable stages of human maturation. While some described these stages within individual lifetimes, few have explored the possibility of these stages developing over a span of many lifetimes.[14]

Carl Jung set up a system of identifying different personality types based on the differences in wisdom and attitudes among similar people. Jung's system is still used by human resource professionals to place individuals in appropriate careers.

William C. Menninger championed the notion of emotional maturity, and published a succinct list of criteria for measuring it. Doctor Menninger, with his father and brother, established the Menninger Institute and Foundation in Topeka, Kansas, as well as a number of clinics for treating emotional and psychological issues.

Abraham Maslow, known as the father of modern management, wrote a theory of self-actualization, which he described as "the full use and exploitation of talents, capacities, potentialities, etc."[15] Maslow listed fourteen characteristics of self-actualized personalities, and eight behaviors leading to self-actualization, that might be considered as steps in a process of spiritual enlightenment.[16]

If we consider that each of us is a piece of infinite wisdom that has split off from our original source in order to experience physical existence, the idea that we grow, mature, and become wiser through a series of lives makes sense. Whether we accept the beliefs that we have been banished from heaven because of unacceptable behavior, or think that we were placed on this earth to learn how to live in peace and to gradually return to a godlike state of being, the concept that we are following a course of learning toward enlightenment seems reasonable.

Within our lifetimes, most people experience some level of spiritual and emotional growth.[17] When we are children, we see life with fresh eyes. Everything is new to us. We think and behave with a sense of wonder and absorb knowledge easily, as we learn to survive in this strange environment. We watch how others behave and learn to interact with our families, with our friends, and with strangers.

As we move into our teen years we begin to strut our stuff. Teenagers sense that they have the world by its tail, and that they know everything they need to know. They drive their parents and teachers to distraction, and lose patience with adults who insist on making everything so complicated and difficult. The German psychologist Erik Erikson described this as the stage of life during which people develop a sense of self and personal identity.

In their young adult years people often strive to establish themselves in society. They work hard to acquire the wealth, material goods, and social standing that they admire in others. By middle age, most workers step back a bit to consolidate and enjoy their gains. They begin to help others more, starting with their own children who are now working to make it on their own.

As people move into retirement, they often downsize, trading the dwelling where they raised their families for a more manageable place close to the people and activities they most enjoy. They shed many of their material possessions and share their experience and wisdom with younger generations.

The concept of reincarnation holds that, just as we mature emotionally and intellectually through each lifetime on earth, our souls mature spiritually through a long series of physical lives. At each stage of development toward spiritual enlightenment, our attitudes and behavior exhibit different characteristics, much as they do when we mature from child to teen to adult. We are all on the same path to enlightenment, but we are not all at the same place on that path. Some of us have lived many more lives than others and acquired more insight and wisdom.

Soul Ages

Michael tells us that during our many lifetimes we progress through five stages of soul development. These are called Infant Soul, Baby Soul, Young Soul, Mature Soul, and Old Soul. There are also two levels beyond Old Soul, known as Transcendental Soul and Infinite Soul. Souls at these two levels rarely materialize on earth, but many Transcendental Souls are now living among us to help with the transition to the new way of thinking and living. Michael says only a handful of Infinite Souls have materialized here. They include Jesus Christ, the Buddha, Krishna, Lao Tsu, and Mohammed.

The following paragraphs describe some of the most typical behavior patterns of individuals at various stages of soul development. These are highly simplified profiles intended only to introduce the concept of soul ages. They are not meant in any way to be judgmental or patronizing. Far more detailed descriptions of soul age characteristics, including the seven levels of development within each soul age, can be found in the Michael material, from which these profiles are derived.

Infant Souls come into this world with little or no experience with physical existence. As a result, they tend to be frightened, confused, and overwhelmed by life. These newcomers seldom appear in highly civilized societies, preferring to begin their earth experience in more primitive cultures.[18] They typically project an aura of innocence and childlike behavior that they do not outgrow when they become adults.

When Infant Souls are born into more advanced societies, they often lead brief, violent lives that frequently end in prison. If you read of a person who has committed a murder or other serious crime but does not seem to understand why they have been arrested, that person is most likely an Infant Soul.

There are relatively few Infant Souls living in the world now. When they were predominant thousands of years ago, society was composed mostly of family groupings or small clans. Their focus was on survival in an alien environment and learning to live with other people. As the average level of enlightenment of the world's population matured over the centuries, the Infant Souls did the menial and repetitive work in society, seldom participating in business or government. Occasionally we see an Infant Soul in modern society. He or she will be characterized by a stunning cluelessness and a bewildered "deer in the headlights" look.

Baby Souls prefer to lead orderly and controlled lives. Like teenagers, they often think they know it all and are especially happy when they can order and control others. Baby Souls prefer the simpler life of small towns over the chaos of life in large cities. They tend to see the world in terms of either/or and seldom recognize or understand life's complexities and nuances.

For Baby Souls things are right or wrong, good or evil, and black or white with no shades of gray between extremes. To a Baby Soul you are either with him or against him. One effect of this type of thinking is that Baby Souls tend to make poor decisions. They will typically define problems into either/or terms, eliminating any nuances or secondary effects of their choices. As a result, their solutions often create more problems and unintended consequences.

Baby Souls can frequently be found in the military or working as police, security guards, and bureaucrats. They thrive in fundamentalist churches and conservative political movements, and stick doggedly to their beliefs even in the face of overwhelming contrary evidence. Although most Baby Souls are decent hardworking people, when placed into positions of authority, they can be mercilessly cruel. They also tend to fail miserably in these positions and do not understand what went wrong. Richard Nixon, Idi Amin, Moammar Gadhafi, and most of the other recently deposed Arab despots, are examples of Baby Souls in positions where they were over their heads with authority.

Young Souls are the go-getters of society. Like young adults, they tend to be hardworking, competitive, driven, and materialistic. They tend to obsess over money and frequently become wealthy—or behave as if they were—and look down on people who are not as hardworking, competitive, driven, and successful as they are. Young Souls like to congregate in big cities and advanced societies.

Young Souls can be ruthless in business and sports and do not seem to understand the concept of compassion. Their actions might severely hurt or destroy the lives and dreams of the people they use or victimize, but they justify their actions as victories over competitors who should simply suck up their losses and move on. They find it difficult to accept responsibility for the consequences of their actions. It's not that they are irresponsible; their brains simply are not wired to understand the effect their actions have on others.

Young Souls dominate the entertainment field as producers, advertisers, and consumers, but not as writers or actors. They are not known for creativity, but rather as imitators who find ways to make money from the ideas of others. Young and Baby Souls combined have comprised a majority in most Western societies in recent centuries. They are responsible for the industrial revolution and the emphasis on material goods that has been the driving force of our consumer economy and our manner of living. The bankers and brokers who nearly destroyed the world economy in recent years are almost universally Young Souls.

Mature Souls experience life on a highly emotional level, often leading lives filled with drama and angst. This is the level of development where souls become aware of the feelings of others and how their own actions influence the behavior and well-being of everyone around them. They tend to be inquisitive about all aspects of life and culture, which leads them to pursue extensive education and social experimentation. Mature Souls tend to be compassionate and actively involved in social causes. Unfortunately, their zealousness and emotional involvement sometimes create more confusion than positive results.

Mature Souls are highly introspective and creative, so they are often the innovators and initiators of social programs and peace movements. Politically, Mature Souls tend toward progressive and liberal policies, but typically cannot seem to figure out the best ways to make these policies work in the real world. President Barack Obama is a Mature Soul. As Mature Souls gradually displace Young Souls in world governance, the prospect of true world peace could become reality. The United States and Canada are now seeing Mature and Old Souls beginning to outnumber Young and Baby Souls.

Old Souls are the teachers, though they are more often found in the garden than in the schools. Like many older adults, they seem to younger souls to be loners and are often considered to be cranks or oddballs. They radiate an inner peace and wisdom, while showing little interest in money, material things, and beating anybody at anything. They rarely aspire to positions of power or wealth, but they can often bring much needed enlightenment to such positions. Abraham Lincoln is a prime example of an Old Soul, thrust into a key position, who changed the world.

Old Souls typically think as progressives but show little interest in convincing others to follow their liberal views. They seem to be happy and remarkably serene, whether living in a solitary manner or in crowded urban neighborhoods where there are many opportunities to hang out with friends who think as they do. Old Souls continue to appear in primitive societies as mentors to Infant Souls, a role they have filled throughout history.

As we gradually move from a culture dominated by Young Souls to one led by Mature Souls, we will increasingly learn to appreciate the wisdom and experience of the Old Souls among us. Just as young adults often ignore—or fail to appreciate—

their elders, Young Souls have little patience with the complex thinking and perceived stodginess of Old Souls. Iceland and Holland are among the few countries currently dominated by Old Souls. It will be many more generations before Old Souls make up more than a small minority of the world's population.

What This Means Now

Of all the personal characteristics described in the Michael material, the concept of soul ages has been the most useful to me. It has helped me to understand why people think and behave the way they do. As a result, I have been able to relate more appropriately to others, focusing on their positive attributes rather than on our differences. After more than two decades of working with this knowledge I can now pretty consistently determine a person's soul age by looking at their eyes and other physical features, seeing how they dress, listening to their political and religious attitudes, or even seeing what sort of vehicle they drive.

The youngest souls are the most clear-eyed, but often exhibit blank looks as if there is nobody home behind the lens. Baby Souls tend to look as if they are wearing blinders, not wanting to see the whole picture, while Young Souls frequently have a furtive or anxious look, as if not trusting anybody or anything. Mature Souls tend to display tired eyes, as if the weight of the world were on their shoulders, which it often is. The oldest souls carry in their eyes a look of deep wisdom, even when they are babies or young children.

My own observations over the years are that Baby Souls tend to have soft, plump faces, dress conservatively, and drive plain vanilla sedans, minivans, and pick-up trucks—a lot of pickup trucks. They are big spectator sports fans, especially of dangerous or violent sports like football, hockey, and automobile racing. They identify very personally with their favorite teams, although older Baby Souls seldom participate in such games themselves.

Young Souls, on the other hand, often work hard at keeping physically fit, and enjoy non-team competitive sports like tennis, golf, and handball. What other people are thinking is very important to them. They like designer clothes and flashy or expensive foreign cars. Young Souls frequently travel to exotic places. They tend to be overly focused on money, investments, and the cost of everything.

Mature Souls, by comparison, are more likely to keep physically fit through individual activities such as hiking, bicycling, cross-country skiing, paddling, and gardening. Mature Souls prefer clothing made from natural materials, houses they build or design themselves, and organic foods. They drive Swedish and German cars, or Japanese hybrids, and tend to keep their vehicles a long time. Old Souls, if they drive at all, will have an old car or small truck. They wear their clothes out and usually avoid physical activities other than work, which they typically do quietly and well.

I now know better than to disagree with a Baby Soul on any subject or issue, especially if it involves sports, politics, or religion, as people at this level identify strongly with their beliefs and take disagreement as a personal attack. I try to avoid being caught up in emotional webs with Mature Souls, as they can be depressing, although I enjoy sharing creative ideas and projects with people at this level. I do enjoy the company of Old Souls, though, realizing that they are not lazy or slovenly, but have simply moved past caring about material success or what other people think of them.

Another personal observation is that there appears to be a relationship between soul age and the ability to comprehend complex problems and ideas. This, of course, remains only speculation at this point, as it has not been tested or proven by a scientific community that does not yet acknowledge the concept of soul ages.

Irrespective of their intelligence or level of education, Baby Souls will try to define complex concepts into choices between two alternatives. Infant Souls might simply change the subject, not recognizing the importance or the complexity of the discussion. Young Souls look at every issue through the lens of how it will affect them personally, without regard to the effect it may have on others. They might also look for ways to use the issue at hand to gain competitive advantage over others.

Mature Souls revel in complexity and often contort the simplest issues into complex problems. They will explore every aspect of an idea or issue but might have difficulty finding a workable solution to a complicated problem without making it worse. Old Souls not only grasp complex ideas but often know the way to solve problems or capitalize on innovative ideas. They will rarely volunteer their thoughts, however, knowing that younger souls will neither understand nor appreciate them.

An example of this phenomenon can be found in the current political discourse. A few Infant Souls have emerged as ultra-conservatives in high elective offices in the United States and several European countries. You can recognize them by their unusually clear eyes and frequent looks of utter bewilderment when presented with complex ideas.

These are bright, articulate individuals who may have achieved success in business or professions, but often respond to complex issues with a naïve simplicity that keeps the comedians and political cartoonists busy. They have become an embarrassment to many of their conservative colleagues, who are overwhelmingly Young or Baby Souls.

The current extreme polarity of political positions; the increasing disparity between rich and poor; and the emerging conflicts between those in power and those without, are all rooted in the difference in thinking and behavior of people at different soul ages. So too are changing attitudes toward police and military. Both were long considered to be beneficial and protective forces, but are now becoming seen to be brutal and destructive. Baby and Young Souls are clinging desperately to old institutions and mores, while Mature and Old Souls struggle to introduce more progressive thinking into politics, religion, and business.

Beyond these personal observations I believe that understanding the nature and behavior of people at different soul ages is essential to understanding what is happening in our world today. As each individual progresses toward a more enlightened state, the total population of the planet also progresses. And as each individual thinks and behaves in a more enlightened manner, the total population of the world begins to think and behave in more enlightened ways.

Note that there is no relationship between soul age and intelligence. Older souls are no smarter than younger souls, but they seem to be wiser and have a better understanding about the nature of life and reality. More advanced souls tend to think and act differently from younger souls and hold very different social, political, and religious values.

Neurologists have learned that the reason adolescents tend to make poor decisions and take unnecessary risks is not just from lack of experience but because certain sectors of their brains have not fully developed.[19] Perhaps the same reason applies to spiritual enlightenment. It could be that enlightenment either causes changes in brain structure or results from such changes, which could explain the differences in our beliefs and behavior as we mature spiritually.

Seth taught us that we choose where and when to come into this world before we are born. He said we also choose to associate with souls that we have known or been related to in earlier lives. This may explain why people of similar soul age seem to dominate villages, regions, or countries.

Michael says that the middle area of the United States is dominated by Baby Souls. This could help to explain why this area has long been known as the Bible belt and why these states have been so reliably conservative politically. Michael also notes that Baby Souls dominate many African countries, the Middle Eastern Gulf states, the Caribbean islands, and most Central and South American countries. These are all areas known for totalitarian or theocratic governments, internecine wars, and violent behavior.

The Dark Ages of history were times when Baby Souls were predominant and in charge of world affairs. While Baby Souls loudly espouse concepts of morality and family values, there appears to be a connection between the presence of a majority of Baby Souls and incompetent, corrupt, and non-democratic government and business leaders.

Japan, South Korea, Israel, and Australia are among the countries where Young Souls currently comprise a majority of the population. The United States and Canada are countries where Young Souls have been dominant in recent history, but are now being overtaken by a Mature and Old Soul majority. These are the countries whose economies and cultures have until recently been focused on production and consumption of material goods.

Most of the European countries, including Italy, England, Sweden, and Norway, already have majorities of Mature Souls. These countries are known for having more advanced programs for social justice, equality, and basic services such as housing, education, and health care.

Western society is now moving into an age dominated by Mature Souls. As such, look for government policies and actions in these areas to become more liberal, environmentally responsible, and compassionate toward people at all levels of society. Most of the older souls in these societies are not yet adult, though, so it will take a few more decades for their impact to be fully felt.

Michael says that the biggest challenge that Infant Souls face in life is learning to relate with other people. They tend to behave in antisocial ways without understanding the consequences of their behavior. Baby Souls have generally overcome this problem, but have not yet learned to fully understand and appreciate the concept of compassion. As Michael notes, Baby Souls can be viciously cruel if given too much authority or placed into certain situations for which they are not prepared.

As souls move up through the Young Soul ages, they begin to see how compassion can influence the responses they get from others, and they learn to use it to their advantage. Young Souls, however, still do not feel any true empathy—the capacity to put themselves in someone else's shoes—for others. That feeling first appears in Mature Souls, who Michael says are finally learning about emotions and caring about others.

Doctors know that certain sectors of our brains control various actions or emotions, and that the level of activity in each sector varies between individuals.[20] Michael states this as a factor of soul age development, which would explain how a Young Soul of equal intelligence to a Mature Soul might react differently to emotional stimuli.

Neuroscientist Patricia Churchland, in her book, *Braintrust*, describes the role that the peptide oxytocin plays in a person's behavior.[21] Simply put, the more oxytocin in a brain, the more likely emotions like empathy will show up in behavior. Since the concept of soul ages has not yet been explored by the scientific community, however, we have no way of knowing if there is a connection between brain development or chemistry and soul age.

The relationship between the predominant soul age of a country and the political and social policies and programs of that country are more readily apparent. Nations like Iraq, Iran, Nicaragua, and Mexico that are dominated by Baby Souls tend to be less stable and more prone to violent behavior than are nations like Sweden, Norway, and England that are dominated by Mature Souls.

As individual souls mature and become more enlightened, the ethos and thinking of their groups, societies, cultures, and nations also mature and become more enlightened. Their prevailing attitudes become more compassionate. Thoughtful debate begins to replace fervent dogmatism, and cooperation replaces competition. Similarly, as the entire population of our earth matures and becomes more enlightened, the earth itself reflects this growth.

Here lies the key to understanding an important element of what's happening in our world today. We are now moving into an age of balance between the thinking and behavior of the Baby and Young Souls and the thinking and behavior of the Mature and Old Souls. This transition will continue for a few more generations. The effects can already be seen, however, in the attitudes of world leaders now coming into power, and will accelerate rapidly as the more advanced souls who are now children move into adulthood.

PART II – WHAT'S HAPPENING

Time and Natural Cycles

Albert Einstein taught us that time is not fixed. Metaphysicists agree that time exists only to help us keep order in our lives. Some fundamental elements of time, however, are based on cycles of the universe. These cycles affect our lives in ways humans have studied for centuries but still do not fully understand. Our days are based on one full rotation of the earth around its axis, but we measure hours, minutes, and seconds by arbitrary divisions of the day.

Similarly, we use a twelve-month calendar first created by an ancient Roman emperor, and modified by a Gregorian monk more than 500 years ago, while the thirteen lunar months control ocean tides, menstrual cycles, and emotional moods.

We honor the passing of years, decades, centuries, and millennia, but we know little of the longer cycles that affect our world in extraordinary ways. The path of the earth through our solar system, for instance, affects our behavior in ways that astrologers have studied since the beginning of civilization, but which our current culture does not seem to consider worth watching.

Fifteen hundred years ago, Mayan shamans refined a complex astrological calendar that may have been devised by Aztecs and other Mesoamerican cultures three thousand years earlier. Mayan legend claims the calendar was given to them by a god that they called Itzamna. The Hopi tribe had a similar calendar, which may have been the original source for the Aztec and Mayan calendars.

It is likely that all of these tribes share the same roots. Aztec is a relatively new name for an ethnic group that, according to legend, migrated to Central America from a place north of Mexico, which is where the Hopi reside. Recent genetic studies have shown that all natives of the eastern Pacific coast, from the Aleutian Islands to Patagonia, evolved from the same original source. They speculate that all of these tribes descended from nomads who came from what is now Russia and Siberia.[22]

The Mayan calendar was based on a 260-day period known as a sacred calendar, which coincided in 52-year cycles with their 365-day period called a vague year. The Mayans also knew that every 2,160 years the earth entered a new age, a time of massive shifts in societal attitudes and ways of thinking and living. These ages coincide with the position of the earth within the twelve astrological sectors of the universe, confirming that the Mayans, and their predecessors, were knowledgeable in astrology.

The longest of the Mayan cycles is called the great cycle or long cycle. A great cycle consists of twelve ages and lasts 25,920 years. The current great cycle concludes on December 21, 2012. At that time our sun will cross the equator of the Milky Way galaxy and complete a full orbit of the galaxy, having transited all twelve astrological sectors.[23]

Since the Mayan calendar does not extend beyond this date, some people have concluded that the world will end at this time. There is no basis in Mayan writings or mythology for this assumption. It is no more logical than saying that the world will end on December 31st of this year, because your desk calendar does not go beyond that date.

The Aztecs had a similar calendar and, like the Mayans, did not predict the end of the planet at this time. The Aztecs defined five ages of the world, which they documented on a stone carving known as the Sun Disk. This monolith is about twelve feet in diameter, three feet thick, and weighs about twenty-five tons. It is now on display at the National Museum of Anthropology in Mexico City.

John Van Auken, a director of the Association for Research and Enlightenment in Virginia Beach, Virginia, has analyzed the Aztec Sun Disk and concluded that the fifth age, known as the Age of Change, also ends on December 21, 2012. He claims that Aztec legend says there are two more ages to follow.

The next age predicted by these legends is the "Age of the Spirit of All Living Things". According to Van Auken, we are about to enter a time when we become more aware of the essence of life and regain a sense of spirit and energy rather than physicality and matter. He states that once we regain that sense, we will recover the real power of life and start to awaken to the spirit of all living things.[24]

Anthropologists and engineers currently studying Mayan and Aztec ruins have recently suggested that the ancient calendars should more properly be called calculators. These researchers say that the time intervals of these calendars represent changes in magnetic energy patterns of the earth and its inhabitants.

Until recently, it was widely accepted that Mesoamericans could not have explored the universe because they did not have the glass lenses needed to build telescopes. New research has suggested, however, that they may have used pinhole apertures—like those in the earliest cameras—placed in tunnels bored into the earth's surface to project images of the stars and planets onto cave floors.

To those who have posited that the 2012 date may mark the end of the world, therefore, scholars of both the Mayan and Aztec calendars counter with authoritative arguments that this date marks not the end but the beginning of a new age in which fundamental beliefs and ways of living change radically from the past. Astrologers concur with this assessment, noting that the earth moves on this date into a sector of the universe known as the realm of Aquarius. Readers who lived through the 1960s will recall the popularity of the coming Age of Aquarius during that decade. That may be unfortunate, as it confers an air of ethereal noncredibility to what should have been an early warning of the changes that we are now seeing.

The noted Astrologer Richard Tarnas, in his book *Cosmos and Psyche*,[25] states that an alignment between Uranus and Pluto that began in 2007 and continues through 2020 points to a significant return within our society to cultural aspects of the 1960s. Included among these are rapid social change; technological and scientific advances; progressive political movements; feminist, civil rights, and countercultural activity; an increased drive for freedom and autonomy at both individual and collective levels; environmental activism; changes in global balance of power; and the awakening of natural instincts.

Tarnas describes his findings of strong correlations between these cultural attributes and the same Uranus/Pluto alignment throughout history. He also documents other astrological connections that indicate major changes in the way we think and behave, both individually and as a society, coming soon to our world.

What this all adds up to is that serious astrologers and the ancient calendars tell us we are about to experience the midpoint in time of a fundamental shift in our thoughts, actions and beliefs. This shift is massive, powerful, and has been predicted for centuries. It is a change that happens only once in twenty-six thousand years. It may not be a mere coincidence that we are moving from a culture dominated by Baby and Young Souls to a culture dominated by Mature and Old Souls at the time of this shift.

At the same time we must adjust to living on a planet that is also changing. The planetary changes are apparently needed to accommodate our new ways of thinking, living, and acting, and to adapt to our new reality. It will take some adjustment, however, for us to learn to live with the new weather patterns; new physical laws; and possibly even seeing new varieties of the human species appearing in our world.

Our World Is Changing

For more than fifty years, meteorologists, geologists and other scientists have been recording strange activities in our planet. Damaging weather in the form of droughts, tornadoes, typhoons, blizzards, hurricanes, floods, and wildfires have recently become more frequent and more severe than they have historically been. Often these disasters have been occurring in areas where they were rare or unknown in the past, such as the earthquakes in India and Italy. Ocean temperatures have risen dramatically, and there has been unusually rapid melting of the polar ice caps and glaciers.

The increased ocean temperature has also raised sea levels slightly because of the expanding volume of the water as it warms. Melting of the polar ice caps will raise sea levels even further. Current estimates call for an increase in average sea level ranging from three feet to twenty feet or more by the end of this century.[26]

The rise in ocean temperature has already begun to alter the movement of major air and ocean currents that influence the earth's weather, including the high altitude jet stream, the Atlantic Ocean Gulf Stream, and the Pacific coast El Nino and El Nina currents. These air and water movements drive weather patterns and have become more erratic and less predictable in recent years. As a result, estimating and predicting the frequency, intensity, and potential paths of major storms has become more difficult.

In the past few years, meteorologists have seen an increase in both the number and severity of hurricanes in the Atlantic Ocean, but the storms have tended to more often track into the Gulf of Mexico than up the eastern coast. In 2008, they recorded the first year that five consecutive named storms hit the U.S. mainland and the first time that four storms of the season were classified as major hurricanes. In 2010 they logged the most active Atlantic Ocean hurricane season ever recorded.[27]

Earthquakes have been occurring more frequently, not only along known major fault lines, but also in areas where they would not normally be expected. Major earthquakes in the ocean floor have caused more catastrophic tsunamis, or tidal waves, than were previously known. In the 142 years between 1850 and 1992, severe tsunamis in the Pacific Ocean occurred on average only once every twelve years. In the twelve years between 1992 and 2004, however, eight severe tidal waves were recorded, averaging one every eighteen months.[28]

Volcanic activity has also increased, and volcanologists have warned that several long-dormant areas are overdue for eruption. We have already seen new activity in Alaska, Chile, Japan, Indonesia, and Iceland. Mounts Rainier, Saint Helens, and Hood in the Cascades; the Yellowstone Park caldera; and Mount Etna are being monitored.

Severe droughts and ferocious wildfires too are being recorded in more regions, covering more area, and happening more frequently than ever before. Australia has recently suffered not only an extended drought and severe wildfires, but also unprecedented inland flooding. In traditionally temperate climates, such as the United States and Europe, summer months have become hotter and winter months have become colder. All these phenomena have been attributed by scientists to global climate change that could foretell the coming of another ice age like the one recorded in the thirteenth century.

Most perplexing of all, perhaps, have been changes in the earth's magnetic field. This is an area of science that remains largely unknown to most people and continues to puzzle even experts in the subject. We do know that birds, fish, insects, and animals have magnetic sensors within their brains that assist migratory species with navigation and that may influence the way they think and act. The recent spate of whales, dolphins, and sea turtles beaching themselves on Cape Cod and other coastal projections may be due to shifts in the magnetic grid that guides their migratory path.

Between 1992 and 2004 the earth's North Magnetic Pole moved farther than ever recorded in a similar period, sliding from northern Canada nearly into Siberia.[29] The North Magnetic Pole is the location to which magnetic compasses point. It is not coterminous with the geographic North Pole, which is the pivot point around which the earth turns. The difference between the magnetic pole and the geographic pole is called magnetic declination.

Magnetic declination varies depending upon where it is measured. Declination changes continuously, but slowly, over time. Navigators used declination charts to adjust their course calculations before the advent of global positioning satellites. In recent years declination has changed far more dramatically and more quickly than usual. One immediate effect of this change is that airports all over the world have had to renumber their runways, which are identified by their magnetic compass headings.

We have a tendency to think of ourselves as being separate from our earth since we are able to move freely about and are not physically attached to the soil. If we instead think of ourselves as individual bundles of energy that are connected to the energy of the planet by the magnetic attraction of gravity, however, we get a better idea of our personal connection to the earth.

We may be more connected to our planet than we realize. We know that this connection is not physical because we are obviously separate and have even flown into outer space. Scientists still do not understand, though, how gravity actually works to keep us attached to the ground. While there may not be a physical connection between our bodies and our planet, there is certainly some sort of energy connection, and this energy connection may affect our thinking as well as our movement.

The strength of the earth's magnetic field has also been dropping, leading some scientists to suggest that it may be ready to reverse itself.[30] Geologists have found through examination of magnetic ores that the polarity of the earth has reversed at least fourteen times over the eons of its existence and that a reversal of polarity has always been preceded by a drop in intensity of the magnetic field.

Note that when the poles reverse, the earth does not flip end for end. Despite the claims of some fear-mongers, that has never happened. If it did, the earth would probably disintegrate from the force of the move. If the magnetic grid reversed, it would severely disrupt communications systems and play havoc with air and sea navigation, but there would be little or no physical change that we would notice.

All of these events signal a fundamental change in the earth's energy. Most of our planet's mass consists of molten rock called magma. At the core is a ball of solid iron. Friction between the iron core and the magma acts as a giant dynamo powering the planet's magnetic grid. The surface has cooled and hardened, forming what we know as solid land, although this surface is relatively thin and most of it lies under the oceans.

The earth's surface is fractured into seven major tectonic plates, a dozen relatively large tectonic plates, and thousands of smaller micro-tectonic plates, all of which float on the core magma. The breaks between tectonic plates are known as fault lines. Earthquakes and volcanic eruptions occur along fault lines when tectonic plates press against or pull apart from each other. These movements of the earth's surface affect air and ocean currents that in turn influence weather patterns.

Geologists and anthropologists tell us that these changes are not unique to our time, but have occurred before. They know that tectonic shifts have caused continents to split, merge, appear, and disappear. That explains why the eastern coast of South America looks like it would match the western coast of Africa. These two continents were once a single land mass.

WHAT'S HAPPENING

The Atlantic Ocean has grown wider as the tectonic plates have separated and the space between them filled with new magma from beneath the surface. At the same time, the Pacific Ocean has grown smaller as its tectonic plates crushed together, submerging lands that once stood above the water.

These global shifts in our physical environment seem to be occurring at the same time as we are seeing global shifts in every aspect of our business, governmental, religious, and personal lives. As the earth's energy shifts, our personal energy is also affected. As our personal energy is affected, we change our attitudes, beliefs, and behavior.

If we assume that there is a fundamental energy connection between us and our planet, and we accept the concept that we are experiencing a mass societal change in thinking and attitudes, then it seems logical to assume that the energy of the planet is also changing in order to enable the new world order that we see evolving. That process of planetary change might help to explain the recent increase in natural disasters and the strange behavior of our weather.

Our planet appears to be renewing itself in preparation for a new age. It may be shaking off some of the abuse we have inflicted upon it during the past few centuries. While the planet is changing, we are at the same time being forced to question our basic institutions, to shed our materialistic obsessions, and to become more compassionate toward each other, recognizing that we are all in this together and facing changes that are beyond our control.

We Are Changing Too

The last few decades have seen rapidly accelerating political changes worldwide. The Berlin wall came down. The Soviet Union collapsed. Dictators have been deposed or co-opted. The Irish have made peace between their religious factions and Ireland briefly became a major player in the world's economy. While the *Celtic Tiger* that emerged has suffered a setback with the world economic recession, the country has matured and changed in ways that could not have been envisioned a generation ago.

China and India have begun to emerge as major world economic powers since embracing capitalistic economic policies and techniques. Western European countries have banded together into a quasi-nation Common Market that, despite recent growing pains, has been so successful that eastern European countries are clamoring to join. Middle-eastern theocracies are being overthrown by populist demands for religious and personal freedom. These economic and political changes have not only been happening more frequently, they have also been happening abruptly, with little or no warning or expectations.

The near collapse of the worldwide economic system in 2008 is likely to be a catalyst that necessitates even more drastic political changes. The world economy is now so interconnected that downturns no longer affect a single country but resonate around the globe. The current situation has already led most economists to question the wisdom of deregulation of money markets by government, and has forced all but the most conservative leaders to acknowledge that some form of government oversight is advantageous.

Totalitarian governments that have built their wealth and power on exploitation of oil resources are beginning to teeter as demand for oil ebbs and new sources of energy are developed. These governments are now facing steep declines in revenue at the same time that they are being pressured to be more open and democratic.

The trend in global politics appears to be toward more open societies, more cooperation with other political entities and less control by governments of their subject populations. Social scientists often attribute the speed of these changes to the advent of television, computers, the Internet, and other recent communications advances.

These technological changes may be part of the shift, however, appearing when they did as catalysts for change. Despotic government leaders have found it much more difficult to maintain control of their subjects since the appearance of satellite television, cell phones, and the Internet. Even before the widespread use of these new technologies, television broadcasts of Western European and American news and entertainment programs may have been a key factor in the collapse of the Berlin Wall and subsequent end of the Cold War by showing residents of Communist regimes how much better life is in democratic societies.

Information that until recently was only available to historians, academics and other research specialists is now readily accessible to anyone with a computer or cell phone and Internet connection, no matter where they are and what their level of education. It is telling that the electronic devices that have so altered the way we do business and conduct our daily routines all became widely popular at first as entertainment media. In the 1930s it was radio, in the 1950s it was television, in the 1980s it was computers. While the earliest computers were intended for business, they did not become widely used until the introduction of personal desktop units only three decades ago.

The frequent advances in computer technology have often been driven not by work and business needs, but by the popularity and demands of computer gaming. It is worth noting that the most popular computer games involve the creation of virtual worlds that replicate real life or fantasy adaptations of real life. This phenomenon may be one more indication of our search for more individual control over our lives and the emergence of an inner knowledge that we have more power over our existence than we have been taught to believe.

Just as computers were originally designed for business but evolved to meet the demands of personal use, the Internet was originally conceived as a military tool and a means for academics to share research, but it has since blossomed into the single most important avenue for personal communication and information sharing ever known.

Today it is personal communication devices such as smart phones and tablets that put our e-mails, text messages, podcasts, music, and videos into our pockets. We no longer have to be hardwired to be connected. We now have constant instant access to each other whether we are at home or at work, and while we are travelling, commuting, vacationing, working, or playing.

As our daily communications have become instantaneous, our more traditional information sources such as newspapers, magazines, and television have struggled, changing formats and downsizing in desperate efforts to survive. These media will probably always be with us, but will evolve into different forms of delivery and importance as a direct result of these global changes.

The election of Barack Obama as president of the United States is a powerful example of the way our society is changing. He was elected not because he is young, black, intelligent, charismatic, or a skilled orator. Some of these characteristics are historical detriments to election. And it was not his message of hope that did it. Obama was elected because of the way he conducted his campaign.

While his political opponents and the conservative media commentators played on the fears and insecurities of the electorate, Obama maintained a serene and confident demeanor that voters found reassuring. As his rivals focused on attacking his weaknesses, Senator Obama treated his opponents with respect. While the Republican candidates spoke fervently about fighting and winning, as if the presidential election were a game between sports teams, the Senator from Illinois quietly laid out thoughtful policies to address the economic and social problems of the country.

Barack Obama used the new communications tools with profound skill. He connected with and energized young voters who had never before paid attention to politics. He used the Internet to raise unprecedented financing, with average donations of less than $100, overwhelming the historic fundraising ability of the Republican Party. Most importantly, Obama conveyed the message that his administration would be based not on fear, competition, and misguided power, but on competent leadership, compassion, cooperation, and caring for all sectors of society.

The press made a big deal of Obama's ethnicity during the campaign and after his election to the presidency. Most of this focus was on the obvious fact that the United States had reached a level of enlightenment that allowed a person of color to win a strong majority of the popular vote and rise to the highest elected position.

Of far more importance, however, is the effect that Obama's election had on the attitudes of African-Americans and other minority groups. Here is a mixed-race individual, raised primarily by grandparents in modest financial circumstances, who overcame all of the factors that have traditionally hindered success. Excuses will not work any longer. Barack Obama has proven that we live in a true meritocracy where intelligence and diligence can overcome any handicap or obstruction.

As a beacon of the new world energy, however, President Obama has become the target of vilification by those who fear change and are clinging desperately to old ways of thinking and behaving. It is ironic that the one person in a position of authority who understands what's happening in our world is trying to lead a nation where nearly half of the population doesn't seem to get it. His critics and opponents sense that the changes he represents are inevitable. They know they cannot stop the changes but will do everything in their power to delay and alter the outcomes.

Their strength lies in their ability to engender fear in the electorate and, since fear is a tool of the old energy, it will eventually fail to work. The reactionary forces may defeat Obama but there are many others who think as he does now moving into positions of leadership, especially in other countries.

The largest oppressed group throughout the world is women, but this too is changing. We are now seeing women more frequently rising to positions of authority and leadership in both business and government. This was unthinkable a century ago and rare only a few decades back. Golda Meir led the way in Israel, along with Indira Gandhi in India, and later, Margaret Thatcher in Great Britain, but few others followed until recently. We are now no longer surprised to see women heading major corporations or holding high government positions.

While women have succeeded in business by adopting the same hard-driving and arrogant management styles of their male cohorts, such attitudes are not welcome in government. The California election of 2010 proved this by defeating former corporate CEOs Meg Whitman and Carly Fiorina, despite their records of business success and record-breaking spending on their campaigns.

Women are breaking out of traditional subservient roles in all societies. In some of the poorest areas of the world, women have begun to band together, forming cooperatives and using microloans to set up small businesses as a way to provide each other with the most basic goods and services, and break loose from absolute control by their husbands, fathers, and male religious leaders.

Ethics have emerged for possibly the first time in our history as an important element in the success or failure of political and business leaders. While unethical behavior has long been endemic in both business and politics, it was until recently generally accepted as part of the game. That is no longer true. Look at the number of elected and appointed government officials, senior executives, and religious leaders who have been toppled from power by ethical breaches in the last few years.

The failure of businesses whose leaders became too greedy, arrogant, or corrupt was also rare until recently. The collapse of the U.S. savings and loan institutions in 1992 marked the beginning of a change, however. In just the last decade, dozens of major corporations have gone under, been forced to restructure, or been taken over by competitors because of personal excesses in management.

The recent collapse of industries that produce consumer goods—and businesses that distribute and sell those goods—may be more than a temporary glitch in the economic system. Chrysler Corporation, General Motors, and the entire shopping mall industry characterize the old order that cannot survive the transition in their old forms. This is a fundamental change that has been apparent to economists for a long time.

These experts have been tracking the rise of the service economy and the decline of manufacturing, and have warned that there are limits to a consumer economy. The great shift is drastically changing the way we do business. We are buying less and serving more. We are beginning to realize that economic growth is not a perpetual constant that we can rely on.

Not only is ethical management becoming essential to success, but a more cooperative interaction is also required between managers and employees.

The gulf between compensation levels of those at the top and those who produce the corporate income is no longer acceptable. We are also learning, through painful layoffs, buyouts, and readjustments, that multiple layers of middle management are not only unnecessary, but can damage a company's ability to compete by stultifying creativity and retarding response to changing markets.

Production efficiencies that have been enabled by the use of computer technologies and automation have made obsolete the mindless repetition of assembly line work. Machinists, welders, and bolt-tighteners have been replaced by engineers running computers and robots. Demand for factory labor with minimal skills has plummeted, while skilled technicians continue to be in demand. The benefits of increased productivity have mostly gone to owners and investors, however, while workers have been squeezed out of jobs that require only limited skills.

Labor unions no longer hold the power to control management decisions. Individual employees are now negotiating their own terms of employment by offering knowledge and talents that employers need, or else they are moving on in ways that were not considered possible in the past. These changes in employee-employer relations are harbingers of a new way of doing business that is pervading all levels. We may soon see companies that were thought to be too big to fail disappear completely, replaced by more entrepreneurial enterprises.

Perhaps the most important element of change in the labor market that we have seen recently is the fundamentally different values and attitudes toward work held by individuals born in the past twenty-five years. This group now makes up half of the world's population and is beginning to show its effect on business, politics, religion, and social practices in every corner of the globe.

Young men and women coming out of colleges and technical schools today are far more likely to be creative, focused, and driven to improve the human condition than were their predecessors in their parents' and grandparents' generations. They are often less competitive, while being more ambitious at the same time. They are highly focused on individual rights and identities, but less selfish in their goals and dreams.

These young people balk at being chained to a desk from nine to five, but often work late into the night and on weekends because of the personal satisfaction of doing useful and creative work. They refuse to wear any type of uniform, especially suits and neckties, preferring jeans, tees, and sandals to Armani garb.

These new workers thrive when offered flexible hours, telecommuting options, and the freedom to follow their own work styles and methods. They do, however, demand recognition for their work, and recoil at any hint of criticism, an attitude that often aggravates older executives and supervisors.

Young workers welcome opportunities to cooperate with others to achieve common goals, and seldom take competitive advantage over anyone else. They also remove themselves from situations where they are overly controlled or micromanaged. Companies that adjust to these new ways of thinking about work tend to thrive. Most notable among these are the new world leaders in technology and communications, whose senior managers are also relatively young and ascribe to the new work ethic.

Another important area of global change is popular attitudes toward war. Napoleon Bonaparte once stated that waging war was man's ultimate purpose. War may in fact be man's ultimate stupidity. Until the middle of the twentieth century, war was almost universally considered to be a noble endeavor. At the height of the Second World War, nearly every citizen of the civilized world was involved in the war effort in some way. These people, on all sides of the conflict, were motivated by true patriotism and a strong belief in the righteousness of their cause.

These attitudes began to change with the Korean War, and this change in attitudes became widespread during the Viet Nam conflict. At that time, many people throughout the world began to see war as futile and wasteful. While earlier wars were fought to dominate or defend nations and territory, recent conflicts ushered in a new era of war for resources or for political aggrandizement.

The two invasions of Iraq by the United States are perfect examples of war for control of resources. The first Gulf War was a response to Iraq trying to annex Kuwait, a key source of oil imports to the United States. History is beginning to reveal that the second invasion of Iraq was conducted in order to regain control over oil resources that were developed by American oil companies and nationalized by Saddam Hussein.

Similarly, the United States and NATO forces remain in Afghanistan long after Al-Qaida has left because the country contains precious metal ores that are scarce or not found in Western countries. A U.S. government study found that Afghanistan holds vast amounts of iron, copper, cobalt, and gold ore; natural gas; and possibly the largest source of lithium in the world.[31]

The Viet Nam conflict and the wars in Iraq and Afghanistan also produced a new phenomenon. The mere presence of fighting forces from other countries led to the creation or strengthening of insurgent groups that had been either weak or nonexistent before the foreign invasion. By their efforts to defeat an enemy through overpowering force, the Western coalition inadvertently created local underground forces of guerilla fighters that it could not defeat militarily.

Isolated and frequently anonymous terror attacks by organized groups or individuals have recently emerged as a new form of international war. The most militarily powerful governments have been helpless to stop them. The United States' War on Terror not only failed to stop terrorism, but also gave it a form of legitimacy as a way for those with little power to cripple those with much power.

We seem to have let our fear of terrorist attacks cloud our judgment, however, and our governments have overreacted in their imposition of restrictions on personal freedom. While random attacks are indeed frightening, they cannot do enough damage to bring down a government or to cripple an economy as would an all-out war. That texting teen-aged driver living down the street from you is a far greater threat to your safety and well-being than Osama Bin Laden ever was.

Religious affiliations and attitudes are changing too. Surveys of American religious identification done in 1990, 2001, and 2008 by researchers at

Trinity College of Hartford, Connecticut, identified dramatic changes in attitudes of Americans toward organized religions.[32] The most recent survey of more than fifty-four thousand adults found that fifteen percent of Americans claim no religious affiliation. What is notable is that this percentage had nearly doubled since 1990. Despite this sharp increase in non-affiliation, the Trinity survey found only one person in sixty—less than two percent—identified themselves as atheist or agnostic.

It is not that people have abandoned belief or faith in God, but that they have found traditional religious doctrine to be irrelevant and often at odds with contemporary culture. The Trinity survey also found that the percentage of adherents of new religious movements, including Spiritualists, Wiccans, and pagans, has grown faster in the past decade, while membership in mainline Protestant churches has declined. People seem to be searching for spiritual connections but not finding them in the traditional places and organizations.

The behavior of some church leaders has certainly contributed to this change in attitudes. Reports of televangelists preaching austerity but living lavishly on parishioner donations; advocating family values while cheating on their spouses; and being caught in homosexual trysts after declaring that homosexuality is a sinful personal choice, raise serious questions about their spiritual integrity.

The Roman Catholic Church has been shaken by the scandal of priests abusing children, then being protected by church elders. Evangelical Christian churches have fired ministers who studied biblical history and realized that, although the bible may have been divinely inspired, its books have been so altered by men over the centuries that they cannot be considered the literal word of God.

The public image of traditional churches seems to be shifting away from the moral authority upon which they have always stood. Most of us want to believe in God, but we are beginning to mistrust our religions and the images of God that they portray. A study published in April 2009 by the Pew Forum on Religion and Public Life found that:

> "Many people who left a religion to become unaffiliated say they did so in part because they think of religious people as hypocritical or judgmental, because religious organizations focus too much on rules, or because religious leaders are too focused on power and money."[33]

It seems that some long-established religions have moved away from their original teachings of brotherhood and compassion. They advocate warfare and retribution, support killing in the name of God, and cling to outdated moral values that do not fit the realities of the world today and are not supported by their own original teachings.

The more fundamentalist branches of some religions appear to have completely abandoned the original teachings of their prophets and to have become the last bastions of hatred, intolerance, and hypocrisy. During these times of economic and social stress in our society, people crave solace from their religious heritages but find cold comfort in the messages that they are getting.

As the world's population becomes increasingly enlightened spiritually, the religious institutions that have traditionally promoted enlightenment may find themselves so entwined in obsolete traditions that they no longer serve any useful purpose. Most people inherently know that there is more to life than that which they can see and touch, but they have not yet found a way to connect with their higher selves and with a personal God that they can trust.

A New Way of Thinking

After extensive study of these societal changes I have identified six fundamental shifts emerging in the way our world's population thinks and acts.

While you might be tempted at first to dismiss the shifts as passing trends or popular fads that come and go without making a lasting difference in our lives, I think they may be here to stay. Examples of each have been appearing in news reports with increasing frequency. When taken together, I think they point to a new level of maturity and enlightenment of the majority of the world's people.

The first shift is a rise in personal independence. People of all ages throughout the world are thinking and acting more independently. They are no longer willing to accept without question what they have been told by their parents, their teachers, or their political and religious leaders.

People are more likely to question authority and to test reality for themselves. As a result, it is becoming more difficult for individuals, governments, or groups to control the behavior and thinking of others. This does not mean people are becoming selfish, however. To the contrary, as we learn to take care of ourselves, we also learn that the rise of individual rights carries with it a corresponding rise in individual responsibility, and we become more concerned with taking care of others.

This shift in thinking is affecting every facet of our lives. It is changing the way we are governed and the way we relate to government at all levels. It is leading us to question traditional religious doctrine and to look deeper into the original teachings of the prophets for spiritual guidance. Finally, and perhaps most important, this shift is affecting how we relate to each other as co-workers, neighbors, friends, family, and intimate partners.

The power of groups such as labor unions, political parties, and special interests has declined, and factions within the ranks of these organizations have increased. An example of this can be found in the ultra-conservative movement known as the Tea Party in the United States. It presents itself as a unified group, but any analysis of its policies and purposes will find no consistency beyond a common frustration and anger that something is not right and needs to be radically changed.

The Tea Party representatives are fracturing the established Republican Party and its tradition of moving in lockstep solidarity to advocate its conservative platform. The Democratic Party, at the same time, cannot seem to agree among its members on how to pursue its goals, or even to agree on what those goals are. All of these groups, on both sides of the aisle, are fading from importance and could eventually disappear.

The second shift is the revelation of secrets and the demand for integrity in all aspects of our lives. In the last few years we have seen an unprecedented number of improper activities exposed in the highest levels of business, finance, religion, and government.

At first glance it may seem that abandonment of honesty and integrity is a sign of moral decay resulting from a more permissive society. Further investigation is likely to find, however, that these activities may actually be less common now than they have been in the past. Such behavior has long been covered up or ignored, but now it is being exposed and condemned.

Sexual impropriety and selling of power by government leaders have been recognized, but largely ignored, for millennia. Stunning mismanagement of corporations and manipulation of the financial markets for personal gain has affected the lives of every person. Child abuse in the Catholic Church was known at the highest levels and covered up for generations. Hypocrisy, prejudice, and intolerance have shaken the roots of evangelical churches and caused a major split in the traditional Anglican Church.

The rise of Wikileaks represents an entirely new phenomenon in public discourse. In the past, small bands of people have caused major disruptions to the established order. Their motivations have typically been political, religious, or financial. Some have simply been irrational. None before have been motivated, however, solely by the desire to change the whole system of the way we think by exposing the hidden behavior behind the operations of supposedly free, open, and democratic governmental organizations.

The new revelations might eventually wipe out the secrecy and deceitful practices that have been ignored or covered up until now. They could take down totalitarian governments, religious hierarchies, and entire industries, not through devious means but by leading them to self-destruction through exposure of their own behavior. The future is not promising for the secretive old ways of developing natural resources, managing insurance and financial markets, or selling tobacco and pharmaceuticals.

The third shift is a move from competition to cooperation in all our affairs. Competition in business, government, and personal relationships is being replaced by cooperation, with startlingly positive results. Competition, as we have traditionally defined it, requires that there be winners and losers; cooperation results in winners on all sides.

One example that has affected us all is the telephone and electric companies. Free market economists argued that increasing competition among utility providers would lead to lower prices. When the United States government eased its regulation of the telephone and electric companies, however, consumer costs more than doubled and service quality dropped dramatically.

When they were forced to compete directly with each other, electric companies stopped cooperating and sharing information. As a result, blackouts that might have affected only a local area in the past have, on several occasions, spread over large areas and even crossed international borders.

During the nineteenth century, competing interests built parallel railroads across several of the world's developed countries. Many of those now-abandoned rights of way were later used for electricity distribution lines. You can still follow them today when you fly. In every case, one of the railroads lost out in competition to the other, resulting in an enormous waste of resources.

During the final decades of the twentieth century a similar duplication of resources installed parallel fiber-optic cable grids to handle anticipated growth in communications. Now many of those cables lie unused, and the companies that did remain in the business are forming new cooperative alliances in an effort to reduce costs and improve efficiency.

There will still be incentives and rewards for individuals and companies that come up with new ideas and systems for increasing production, efficiency, and profits, but they will not be based upon beating or destroying the abilities of other individuals or companies from doing the same things. Imagine the possibilities that will come when the most brilliant and creative minds in business and finance cooperate to solve problems now facing our world. By working together to provide the goods and services that we need, all will benefit, especially consumers.

Sports and games will have to change too, and that may not be a bad thing. Think of how much incentive children will have to excel in physical activities when they are no longer taught at an early age that only the best are winners and that even the second best are branded as losers. No longer will there be rewards for the best and failure for everybody else. We have been taught that war-like competition is essential to the advancement of society and to spur creative thinking in business and government, but we are now learning that such competition may actually retard growth.

The movement toward greater cooperation will not diminish the natural human desire for recognition and accomplishment, however. It will instead provide more incentive for individual accomplishments and entrepreneurship. We have all been taught that competition encourages people to try harder. Personal recognition and rewards, though, are bigger incentives to innovation than is beating out somebody else. That may be the key to this change: we might be moving toward a system that encourages innovation and growth, but not couched in the language or intent of making losers out of others who are trying to do the same thing.

The fourth shift is a balancing of masculine and feminine energy, where women and men reach parity in authority and power. Anthropologists tell us there were times in the ancient history of our world when women ruled society in all its aspects, while men did the hunting, gathering, and other drudgework. In more recent history, of course, we have seen those roles reversed, although the hunting and gathering is now more often done at the mall or market than in the fields and forests.

For at least the past four thousand years, men have ruled all aspects of society, from the lowliest households to the grandest empires, including business, religion, and government at all levels, while women have generally been relegated to subservient roles. That is now changing. There are some notable exceptions, of course. Women have in past centuries ruled England, France, Germany, Russia, and other dynasties, but in each of these situations, the women ruled as men did, with belligerent and vicious authority.

Women who are now moving into positions of high authority are no less strong, but they are bringing more intrinsically feminine traits to their leadership. They are employing compassion instead of fear, cooperation instead of competition, and discussion instead of belligerence. Under the new world order, women will not be taking over all the leadership and power, but I envision them assuming an equal position with men in society.

Government policies and actions will continue to be more thoughtful and inclusive as the balance between men and women in power becomes equal. This balance will be deeper and more complex than simply countering male ego with female passion. We are already seeing the behavior of men in power becoming more caring and the behavior of women in power becoming more confident.

The next President of the United States is as likely to be a woman as a man. That would have seemed ludicrous only a decade ago, but is obvious today. We are no longer surprised to see women heading large corporations, government agencies, and universities. Gender differences simply will not be part of the discussion when the younger generation now coming into power chooses individuals for positions of authority.

The importance of the move to gender equality goes far beyond the issue of fairness and balance; it means that government and business leadership in the future is likely to be less belligerent and more compassionate than it has been during the reign of the males.

The fifth shift is toward a society motivated more by compassion than by fear. For most of recorded history, we have seen interpersonal conflicts that resulted in cruelty ranging from mean-spiritedness to all-out war. The root of this cruelty is always a sense of fear. We fear that somebody else might get something that we cannot have or that was not properly earned. We fear that others will take what we have earned. We fear that we might look bad if somebody else looks good.

These fears often constrain people from sharing their talents and assets with others who need them. As we gradually learn to set aside our fears, both as individuals and as societies, we will become more compassionate toward the needs and concerns of others. When we replace fear with compassion and competition with cooperation, a very different society will emerge.

As this is being written the world is watching suppressed people in Mediterranean countries throwing off their fears and challenging the tyrants who have kept them in a state of perpetual fear for decades. At the same time, the United States, Canada, United Kingdom, and the European countries seem to be cowering in fear of everything from immigrants to terrorists. Governments in all of these countries are being forced into reactionary and isolationist positions by increasingly fearful and conservative electorates.

I believe what we are seeing is new world energy rising and old world energy fading. This is a clear trend that should overwhelm the old guard very soon, bringing new leaders to the world stage—leaders who are not frightened by the old myths and habits, and who understand the promises of the new energy.

Ironically, the major tragedies we have experienced in recent years have served at least one positive purpose by increasing compassion among those who were not directly affected. The Indonesian tsunami and Indian earthquake of 2004; the devastation of New Orleans and the Gulf Coast by Hurricane Katrina in 2005; the Myanmar cyclone of 2008; and the Haitian earthquake of 2010 all generated compassionate reactions worldwide. While government response to these events was universally inept, individuals generously shared money, skills, and time to aid recovery.

The destruction of New York's World Trade Center by Saudi terrorists resulted in a dramatic change in attitudes and behavior throughout the city. While each of the five boroughs of New York have always had strong neighborhood identities, they have never before seen the kind of cohesive feeling those neighborhoods now share with each other as a result of their united reaction to the tragedy of September 11, 2001.

Finally, and perhaps the most important because it influences all the other changes, the sixth shift is a fundamental change in attitudes among a majority of the world's people and their leaders. Half of the planet's population today is younger than twenty-five, but nearly all of the world's leaders in government, religion, and education, are much older. The fastest growing businesses, though, are run by surprisingly young entrepreneurs. Some of these new leaders are beginning to bring their enlightened management styles into government. This trend could accelerate as the older leaders are forced out, retire, or die off.

These six changes are affecting all aspects of our society and dramatically influencing world affairs, social interactions, and our interpersonal relationships. Look for the effect of these shifts to become stronger very quickly over the next few years. The old ways and attitudes will not suddenly disappear. The changes will be subtle and are likely to take generations before they are fully integrated into our thinking and behavior.

As the current generation of more enlightened children mature and move into positions of power and authority, they are changing the way business and government perform. Their attitudes are changing policies and their examples are changing the attitudes of those around them.

President Barack Obama is a perfect example of this phenomenon. Whether you agree with his policies or not, note how he differs from his predecessors in both Republican and Democratic parties. He gets it. Unfortunately, he is trying to lead a nation that lags behind the rest of the world in understanding the importance of the changes that we are now experiencing.

President Obama understands what's happening to our world and is a key player in the change. Look at the following words and phrases he used in his January 2009 acceptance speech and compare them to the fundamental changes described above:

"We have chosen hope over fear,"

"What the cynics fail to understand is that the ground has shifted beneath them."

"We cannot help but believe that the old hatreds shall someday pass; that the lines of tribe shall soon dissolve; that as the world grows smaller, our common humanity shall reveal itself; and that America must play its role in ushering in a new era of peace."

"To those who cling to power through corruption and deceit and the silencing of dissent, know that you are on the wrong side of history."

"The world has changed, and we must change with it."

Shedding the Old Ways

Our world has indeed changed, and some people are changing with it. Others are desperately grasping for any way to hold on to a simpler past. Not that the past was better but because it is known. We tend to remember the good things of the past and forget the bad. I see a clear trend emerging, though, between the old and new ways of thinking.

The growing separation is most apparent in the political realm. The extreme divide between political conservatives and liberals occurring worldwide is no accident. As frustrating as it may be to adherents of both sides, this rift is entirely appropriate and necessary in order for us to finally abandon the old ways and embrace the new ways of thinking and acting.

The old political institutions and ways of doing business must collapse from their own behavior and lack of relevance before they can be replaced by new systems. They cannot be simply pushed aside because they would then continue to exist and influence the way we think and act.

The old energy is based on fear. It nourishes selfishness, hatred, bigotry, greed, and secrecy. It allows manipulation and control of the many by the few, whether in business, government, or religion. It reinforces the image of differences between people based upon skin color, race, religion, national origin, education, and economic status. It thrives on lies and domination of the weak by the strong. It has brought us poverty, suffering, crime, war, and economic disparity. It is thoroughly corrupt.

The new energy is based upon the universal godly quality of love. It nourishes honesty, integrity, generosity, and compassion. It encourages independence and freedom. It thrives on truth, acceptance, cooperation, and sharing. It supports governments that honor and protect the interests of everyone, not just the wealthy and powerful.

When fully realized, the new energy promises universal abundance, equality, and world peace. This is the future we could eventually see, but not until we work through a painful process: the death rattle of reactionary and unenlightened thinking.

During the past decade, conservative governments in the United States, Europe, and the United Kingdom, operating under the old energy ways of thinking and acting, nearly bankrupted their countries. Their belligerent and violent reactions to the threat of terrorism deepened perceived differences between Eastern and Western theologies, causing hundreds of thousands of disaffected men and women to join terrorist causes.

The younger generation of voters came out in force to replace these old-school leaders with new leaders. Conservative politicians and their wealthy backers still control popular television and radio outlets, though, and set out an agenda to vilify and undermine the new leaders.

A frightened electorate, many of whom had lost jobs and homes in the economic collapse, rose up in protest, pushing for reform and ousting many long-time politicians throughout the western hemisphere. Desperately seeking to return to a time in the past that they imagine was without the corruption and incompetence of the present, this group supported candidates who fed on their fears and promised a return to the good old days.

Unfortunately, these reformers are often proving to be even more incompetent and recalcitrant in their positions than the people that they replaced. They will reform government, but not by taking it back to the past. They could instead cripple it completely, which may be their cosmic mission. They are unwittingly destroying the old structure so that that the new leaders can move in. In essence, they might succeed in their mission by failing in their intent.

What other elements of our culture are likely to disappear under the new energy? Here is a short list of the top ten. This is only the beginning. Expect to see other aspects of our society collapse that have always been considered to be infallible.

Constant growth of population. Since the beginning of the industrial revolution in the 18th century, the world economy has relied upon steady growth in population and subsequent growth in demand for resources and material goods. That is now changing. Seth tells us that every soul who has ever lived on earth has come back at this time in order to experience the great shift in our world. That is the reason for the huge surge in world population, which has nearly tripled over the last fifty years.

The rate at which the world's population has been growing has declined sharply over the past two decades, however, and total population may soon begin to decline also. A reduction of the number of people on earth will have profound effects on every aspect of our existence. It will require a complete revision of the way we think about money, work, resources, politics, and the environment.

Environmental degradation. Our earth is now reacting to two centuries of over-exploitation of natural resources and pollution of the environment. The global shift in energy that is creating the storms and other natural disasters is cleansing the surface and setting the stage for renewal.

As old resources such as coal and petroleum become depleted or more difficult to extract, new resources will be discovered, but their development could be expensive and time-consuming. We are learning the hard way that we can no longer plunder the natural abundance of the planet for short-term gains and concentrated wealth.

War and other acts of mass violence. War is obsolete and it has been for some time. We no longer need to have enemies that must be defeated by killing their soldiers and occupying their territory. We are entering a time when the mayhem and brutality of warfare are being replaced by diplomacy and discussion to find new and more peaceful ways to resolve our differences.

For the first time in the history of our civilization, we have the potential to achieve true world peace. As the ability to communicate our thoughts and ideas instantaneously to any location has developed, we can now talk with anybody at any time about any subject. Disagreements will remain, and tribal conflicts will continue for a while, but the new era of communication and cooperation will enable world leaders to work out their issues without resorting to physical confrontation.

Totalitarian government. Throughout the 2000-year cycle that is now closing, and possibly much longer, our world has endured the ravages of governments that dominated and controlled the lives of their people. Even today, more than half of the world's population lives under some form of government-imposed suppression of speech, movement, or other limit on personal freedom. This is about to change. The most obvious effect of the new world energy that we are seeing now is the overthrow of totalitarian leaders, not by invasion or assassination but by popular rebellion.

The invasion of Iraq by the United States, and the multiple invasions of Afghanistan by the U.S., Russia, and a parade of others before them, may have actually delayed the overthrow of the dictators and warlords who control those countries. Only three decades ago every South American country was ruled by a dictator; today only one remains a totalitarian state. None of these new democracies was created by foreign invasion; all arose from internal rebellion. All of these countries also now have strong economies, while the countries that suffered foreign invasions in the name of democracy struggle to recover.

I think we should expect the popular uprisings in the middle-eastern nations to spread in both directions, deposing autocratic regimes across Africa and Asia in the near future. These changes are related to the increase in personal freedom, and the breakdown of controlling authority, that is fundamental to the new world order.

Authoritarian religion. The world's governments have not been the only limiters of personal freedom over the past two millennia. All of the world's major religions have been—and continue to be—as guilty of suppressing the masses of people and enforcing their control over individual behavior and attitudes as have governments.

While the Christian churches no longer control Europe and try to impose their beliefs on colonized nations, and the number of theocratic governments has diminished to a few Muslim countries, a large number of people throughout the free world still follow the fiats of the Roman Catholic Pope.

Many others adhere strictly to the dictates of their religious leaders out of fear for the safety of their souls in a mythical afterlife. The generations that are now moving into adulthood reject this form of control, though, and the traditional churches continue to lose members and authority.

Extreme economic disparity. Throughout all of recorded history, a small minority within every society has enjoyed enormous abundance of wealth, power, education, and material goods. At the same time, the majority of every population has had to struggle and toil to simply survive. The gap between the wealthiest elite and the working masses has become even wider over the last few decades.

That is all about to change. The global shift is bringing down those wealthy and powerful individuals who attained their wealth and power through dishonest, uncompassionate, or unethical means. Those who succeed through honest competency will still be rewarded, though.

More importantly, the new world order promises to raise and empower those who are struggling. Extravagantly excessive wealth and unreasonable power may disappear, but there will still be individuals who have more of everything than they need. There should not, however, be anyone who lacks the basic elements of living that they require to survive in reasonable means.

Paternalistic employment. Most of our parents and grandparents saw work as something you did for someone else, who in turn provided income, insurance, and other benefits, followed by an assured retirement. They tended to stay with a single employer all of their working lives, never considering how a move to a different job might improve their circumstances.

That pattern no longer fits the reality of our changing system, and the younger generations no longer expect this sort of paternalistic employment. Many have seen their parents betrayed by a system that promised lifetime security then reneged on those promises, forcing them to take jobs for which they are overqualified and at deep cuts in pay and little prospect for comfortable retirement.

Workers now realize that they need to watch out for their own welfare. They need to be much more entrepreneurial, making their own arrangements for insurance and retirement, and fully expecting that they will have many different employers—and possibly several different careers—over the course of their working lives. They know what they are worth and will not sell out for empty promises. As we move away from an economy based upon the extraction and processing of resources into hard goods, and toward an economy based on service to and support of others, we can expect to see more people working independently or creating their own businesses.

Bigotry and prejudice. Think back to the attitudes of your grandparents. Chances are that regardless of their intelligence, educational level, social standing, or economic status, they held different opinions than you about people who did not share their ethnicity, religion, political affiliation, or nationality. For them, bigotry and prejudice were universally accepted by society. That began to change seventy years ago, when the Germans turned on the Jews and the United States imprisoned American citizens of Japanese origin during the Second World War.

At about the same time, armed forces and sports teams the world over began to recognize the abilities of people of color and integrate them into their ranks. A generation later, in the 1960s, the free world took a leap ahead by adopting laws and policies that made these attitudes politically incorrect, if not illegal.

Today bigotry and prejudice are still found in the elderly, in unsophisticated societies, and among those who never learned to think critically. These attitudes no longer exist in the more enlightened younger generations, however. They will soon die off with their adherents, who find themselves increasingly out of synch with the new world energy.

Secrecy in all its forms. We have entered an age of revelation. Not the revelation defined by the Bible but revelation as defined by Wikileaks. It is a time when all secrets and hidden behavior are exposed. Whether it is government conspiracy, religious duplicity, or personal transgression, the perpetrators are being exposed as never before in our history. People throughout the world are demanding transparency in government, business, and information, and the communications tools we now use are making it impossible to keep the smallest secrets unexposed. Secrecy cannot survive in the new world energy.

Conspiracy and deceit. As secrecy disappears, so too will the conspiracy and deceit that embrace it. These behaviors are about more than secrecy, though. They are about domination and control of money and people. The most egregious deceits that have been uncovered in the last decade are not about government cover-ups of alien invasions or other popular paranoia. They are more likely to involve deceitful business practices that have affected the health, wealth, and well-being of every one of us.

These conspiracies include the tobacco companies that added addictive chemicals to their products while denying the adverse health effects of smoking. They include the gas, oil, and coal companies that conspired with government inspectors to bypass safety rules and standards. And they include the pharmaceutical manufacturers who pay doctors to promote drugs not simply to treat problems, but to prevent rare conditions and counter the side effects of other drugs.

PART III – WE HAVE BEEN WARNED

The New Revelations

Most religious scholars now maintain the importance of revelation, whether received in sacred texts or by personal experience. This theme was first developed by Moslem theologians in the tenth century, and later circulated by Jewish writers. It was then adopted by Thomas Aquinas in the thirteenth century, when he wrote:

> "A revelation from God was necessary for man's salvation, for although these truths may be known by reason, few could attain them and do so without some admixture of errors, and it would have taken a lifetime of thinking, but these saving truths must be known early in life."[34]

Every major religion of the modern world is based upon scriptures and revelations that were delivered to or through human beings from a spiritual entity, either by way of meditation, dreams, or by direct contact. The ancient texts are universally considered to be messages from God. The burning bush that gave Moses the Ten Commandments may have been an energy entity that materialized from the spirit world.

While the ancient texts are widely known, few people realize that similar messages are again coming to us today in the same way. We may not encounter burning bushes that talk, but we are getting messages through personal experiences, dreams, intuition, and through a growing number of people who channel information they receive while in a meditative trance. Maslow called these personal revelations "mystic-" or "peak-experiences".[35]

Religious leaders typically dismiss these new messages because they often conflict with accepted church doctrine and threaten the legitimacy of the established order. We worship ancient texts that we accept were delivered by messengers from the spirit world, while ignoring contemporary texts that are more relevant to us today and may be coming from the same source.

For at least three hundred years, we have been getting spiritual messages through various mediums with increasing frequency and clarity. The best of these teachings are remarkably consistent with each other and with observable experience in our world. Others can be discounted as fraudulent—created by charlatans—just as they were in ancient times.

The twenty-seven books of the Christian New Testament, for example, were distilled from hundreds of potential texts considered by the Council of

Nicea when it compiled the first biblical codex during the fourth century A.D.[36] It took the Council thirty-two years to finally agree on which books to include and which to exclude. According to Professor Bart D. Erdman, this process was often more political than academic, as the Council members excluded works that differed from established church theology. We no longer need a council of religious leaders to decide what we should believe or reject. The new revelations are readily available to every one of us, without being filtered through established institutions.

The new revelations also have the advantage of being immediately transcribed word for word, assuring that we are getting the messages as they were delivered. Professor Erdman tells us that the books of the bible were passed on verbally for as long as a century before being written down. He says they were then transcribed by hand for another two hundred years or more before being codified into the bible that is in use today.

The monks and scribes who copied the documents were often illiterate and therefore not able to read or understand what they were writing. As a result, modern biblical historians have found multiple copies of the same books with lines or whole pages missing, or with conflicting interpretations of the same passages.[37]

Some of the new revelations started coming through more than 200 years ago. In many cases they have been brought out by writers who may have been divinely inspired without knowing it. The following paragraphs describe some of the more credible people and movements that have brought the new revelations to light.

A Colossal Soul

The Swedish engineer, philosopher, and theologian, Emanuel Swedenborg may have been one of the earliest advocates of spiritual study in relatively modern times. Born in Sweden in 1688, Swedenborg became known as a brilliant scientist and prolific inventor. For several years he published a scientific magazine to publicize his works. These included sketches of a flying machine and a submarine, among many other ideas. He also served as Assessor in the Swedish Board of Mines.[38]

When he was fifty-six Swedenborg began to have what he called a conscious perception of the spirit world and its inhabitants. Three years later he resigned his government position, abandoned his scientific inquiries, and devoted the remainder of his life to spiritual studies and writing.

His father, Jesper Swedenborg, was a professor of theology at Uppsala University and known for his unconventional belief that angels and spirits were present in everyday life. Jesper undoubtedly influenced Emanuel's thinking, but it apparently took a while to manifest itself in his work.

What prompted this change, according to Swedenborg, was the experience of being in constant communication with angels from the spirit world. He wrote that he did not physically see or hear these spirits, and never entered a trance state, but saw and communicated with them in his mind, while both asleep and awake. At the time, his contemporaries thought he was crazy and tried to have him declared insane. The Lutheran Church attempted to excommunicate him for his beliefs.[39]

His continued public service and the rationality of his pronouncements led more sensible thinkers to realize that, although he may have been a bit odd, Swedenborg was more brilliant than crazy. Over the next twenty-eight years, he wrote dozens of books, including eighteen theological works in thirty volumes, all of which remain in print.[40]

Three themes pervade Swedenborg's writings. The first is that all of the established religions had strayed from their original teachings and become more interested in money and power over their congregants. The second is that the bible had been distorted and misrepresented by the churches.

The third theme is that there is a relationship between the physical, the spiritual, and the divine worlds that would explain how matter relates to spirit. Swedenborg called this last concept his "correspondence" theory, an idea that is only now being embraced by quantum physicists, who study the behavior of subatomic parcels.

To bolster his argument that the churches had distorted the original meanings and interpretations of the bible, Swedenborg undertook a massive project in which he analyzed the entire bible, verse for verse, translating from the original Hebrew and Greek texts and bringing new interpretations that he claimed were given to him by his angels. His claim that churches "had perished through falsities of doctrine and evils of life" seems as valid today as it was then.

Two Christian church denominations, now known as the Swedenborgian Church of North America and the General Church of New Jerusalem, are based upon his philosophy and teachings. Swedenborg spoke of "The New Church" that would be founded on the theology of his works, but he himself never tried to establish an organized religion.

Swedenborg's most popular and widely read work, *Heaven and Its Wonders and Hell,* was first published in 1757. In keeping with the academic convention of the time, all of his books were written in

Latin. An excellent translation of this book by George F. Dole, more simply titled *Heaven and Hell*, was published in 2000 by the Swedenborg Foundation of West Chester, Pennsylvania. In this book Swedenborg described the afterlife of the soul as not unlike life in this world. His concept of heaven was of a place where souls study, interact with each other, and progress toward an infinite knowledge and understanding.

Swedenborg's description of hell makes a lot more sense than the place of eternal torture and damnation defined by the fire and brimstone preachers of today. His description of the afterlife is shared by modern psychics who also seem to have his ability to communicate directly with the spirit world.

Swedenborg characterized hell as a place where souls go by choice so that they might continue the same sort of uncharitable behavior and thinking that they practiced in life.[41] He allowed for the possibility of redemption and emphasized that souls in hell are isolated from those who choose not to go there. His most convincing argument is simple logic: evil souls would be as uncomfortable in heaven as righteous souls would be in hell.

Ralph Waldo Emerson was strongly influenced by Swedenborg's writings. In his collection of essays on representative men of history, Emerson ranked Swedenborg with Plato, Shakespeare, and Goethe, calling him "A colossal soul ... not to be measured by whole colleges of ordinary scholars."[42]

Emerson apparently never claimed to be in direct communication with angels, but he acknowledged the existence of what he called an over-soul that inspired his thoughts and ideas. His work built upon many of the concepts that Swedenborg espoused and may have been divinely inspired in other ways. The two men held similar beliefs about the nature and purpose of religion in society.

The Dawn of Spiritualism

A quasi-religious movement known as spiritualism began in the United States in 1848 and swept the Western world more as a parlor game than as a serious field of study. This was the first widespread popular recognition in modern times of the possibility that individuals could communicate directly with spiritual entities, including the spirits of dead relatives.[43]

By 1880 this movement had evolved into a sort of religion, with adherents gathering in camps throughout the country. The Spiritualist Church that was established at that time remains active today. Unlike more traditional religions, spiritualism is not based on any scripture or teachings of an ancient prophet. Instead, Spiritualists communicate directly with souls who have left their earthly existences.

Spiritualist Church leaders are typically ordinary people who have developed the ability to sense and interpret the presence of entities from the other side of the veil. Spiritualists profess a strong belief in God, but do not claim any exclusivity in their worship. That is, they do not deny the validity of any other religion or insist that their definition of God is the only valid one. While they do not follow a particular prophet, Spiritualists honor all of the prophets, including those of Native American Indians and other indigenous groups.

A Spiritualist Church service typically includes a sermon based not on scripture but on personal experience, as well as the singing of hymns and sharing of greetings as in many other churches. At the heart of the Spiritualist service, though, are two practices not usually found in the mainline religions: those are healing and mediumship.

Parishioners who desire healing will typically sit in a circle of chairs. Church members who have developed the ability to channel healing energy stand behind them in silence with hands on their shoulders or embracing their heads without touching. The leader may intone healing words, mantras, or songs during this procedure. Those who have experienced this practice say they can feel a warm glow and sense a healing energy flowing through their bodies.

During the mediumship, the leader will approach a member of the congregation and ask permission to summon a spirit. With permission granted, the leader will then describe the physical appearance and personality quirks of the spirit or spirits he or she is sensing. Usually the congregant will recognize the spirit as a relative or a friend who has passed. Often, though, there is no recognition.

The medium will then convey a message from the spirit and conclude with a blessing from spirit. While it would be easy for a cynic to dismiss this practice as pure chance, continued observation will occasionally reveal connections so real and so moving as to make anyone a believer. A skilled medium will convey information that could not possibly be known by a stranger, occasionally including messages from beloved pets that have passed on.

The National Spiritualist Association of Churches puts forth the following Declaration of Principles, not as a creed, but as the consensus of fundamental teachings of Spiritualism:[44]

> We believe in Infinite Intelligence.
>
> We believe that the phenomena of Nature, both physical and spiritual, are the expression of Infinite Intelligence.

We affirm that a correct understanding of such expression, and living in accordance therewith, constitute true religion.

We affirm that the existence and personal identity of the individual continue after the change called death.

We affirm that communication with the so-called dead is a fact, scientifically proven by the phenomena of Spiritualism.

We believe that the highest morality is contained in the Golden Rule: "Do unto others as you would have them do unto you."

We affirm the moral responsibility of individuals, and that we make our own happiness or unhappiness as we obey or disobey Nature's physical and spiritual laws.

We affirm that the doorway to reformation is never closed against any human soul here or hereafter.

We affirm that the precepts of Prophecy and Healing are Divine attributes proven through Mediumship.

Other Enlightened Sources

A similarly enlightened movement known as theosophy is an ancient theological philosophy that claims, as do the Spiritualists, knowledge of the divine gained through personal inspiration and experience. Although theosophy has existed for more than two thousand years, it was not widely known in the Western world until late in the nineteenth century when its concepts were translated and presented in two books by a Russian immigrant to the United States named Helena Petrovna Blavatsky.

Madame Blavatsky lived from 1831 until 1891. She became aware at an early age that she had unusual psychic abilities and was not like other children. She then spent much of her life traveling the globe in a search for spiritual knowledge and wisdom.[45]

After several extended visits to India and Tibet, where she studied under various occult masters, Madame Blavatsky immigrated to the United States in 1873. Two years later, along with several of her mentors, benefactors, and fellow spiritualists, she founded The Theosophical Society, an organization that continues to be active to this day.

The stated purposes of The Theosophical Society are threefold: to form a nucleus of the Universal

Brotherhood of Humanity, without distinction of race, creed, sex, caste, or color; to encourage the study of comparative religion, philosophy, and science; and to investigate unexplained laws of nature and the powers latent in man.

Helena Blavatsky wrote two classic books that remain in print today. *Isis Unveiled*, a two-volume set first published in 1877, combines both science and religion to demonstrate the existence of God and the immortality of the soul. Her second book, also published in two volumes, came out in 1888 after a decade of more world travel and study of Eastern religious concepts. Titled *The Secret Doctrine*, this work translated portions of the *Book of Dzyan*, a Tibetan collection of possibly the world's most ancient religious teachings.

In *The Secret Doctrine*, Blavatsky also attempted to find the common threads among the teachings and tenets of the world's major religions. This effort has become a principal focus of the modern day theosophical community. Two other essential concepts of this movement are reincarnation, including its karmic implications, and the "essential oneness" of all beings. Theosophy teaches that all life throughout the cosmos originates from the same unknowable divine source. Blavatsky's works are difficult to read, leading some scholars to suggest that her thinking may have been influenced by substances other than pure spirit.

One of the most prominent seers of the mid-twentieth century was Edgar Cayce, a man with limited education but extraordinary psychic gifts. Cayce would put himself into a trance after being asked questions, and then awaken with answers. Many of his questioners asked about health problems. His responses often involved simple homeopathic treatments for specific ailments that worked to cure problems for hundreds of people.

Cayce claimed to leave his body and travel to a place where all worldly records are kept in order to obtain his information. This claim is consistent with descriptions by other psychics of a central repository of information, known as the Akashic Record or Hall of Records.

Edgar Cayce died in 1945 but his teachings live on through the work of his Association for Research and Enlightenment, Inc. (A.R.E.). Cayce established this not-for-profit organization in 1931 to research and explore subjects such as holistic health, ancient mysteries, spirituality, dreams, intuition, and reincarnation. Cayce's A.R.E. is based in Virginia Beach, Virginia, and presents conferences and classes throughout the world.[46]

Readers who were alive during the 1960s will remember the hippie movement, with its flower children and their message of peace and love. The Broadway musicals *Hair* and *Jesus Christ, Superstar*, and the rock opera *Tommy*, left some lasting impressions on our society. The movement quickly faded, however, in a haze of pot smoke and hallucinogenic babble. That was unfortunate. The fundamental message of the 1960s presaged the global changes that we are experiencing today. That message is to abandon our fears and embrace love in all that we do.

The 1960s also saw many serious academics and social scientists beginning to share thoughts of a major shift in worldwide attitudes and thinking. Working quietly on their own and in groups that shunned publicity, these brilliant minds published many books that are only now being recognized for their clarity of thought. Aldous Huxley, Alan Watts, Arnold Toynbee, Linus Pauling, Abraham Maslow, Carlos Castaneda, Marshall McLuhan, Buckminster Fuller, and S.I. Hayakawa were all part of this movement.

In 1971, a year after the first Seth book was published, American astronaut Edgar Mitchell was a crewmember on the Apollo 14 moon mission. Dr. Mitchell was a naval air captain, test pilot, engineer, and scientist who saw space exploration as a technological triumph that signified unprecedented mastery of the world in which we live.

On the return trip, Mitchell saw our planet floating free in space and was engulfed by a profound sense of universal connectedness. He later said:

> "The presence of divinity became almost palpable, and I knew that life in the universe was not just an accident based on random processes. The knowledge came to me directly."[47]

Two years later, after searching out others who felt a need for an expanded and more inclusive view of reality than the view that was then held by the scientific community, Dr. Mitchell formed the Institute of Noetic Sciences (IONS). IONS is a nonprofit membership organization based in Northern California that, in its words, "conducts and sponsors leading-edge research into the potentials and powers of consciousness—including perceptions, beliefs, attention, intention, and intuition."[48]

The Institute explores phenomena that do not necessarily fit conventional scientific models, while maintaining a commitment to scientific rigor. IONS describes itself as "... not a spiritual association, political action group, or a single-cause organization, but honors open-minded approaches and multiple ways of knowing, bringing discernment to its work and supporting diversity of perspectives on social and scientific matters."[49]

Until recently IONS published scholarly articles that explore new ways of knowing and being in an excellent quarterly magazine called *Shift*. It also publishes books on related subjects. If you, like many people, remain highly skeptical of psychic mediums and paranormal phenomena, and hold to a "show me" stance on the existence of a more complex world than that which we can see and measure, you may find the IONS programs and publications enlightening.

While their rigid adherence to high academic standards and scientific rigor sometimes seems to limit the extent to which IONS researchers find answers to their questions, it grants them a level of credibility not often found in other spiritual and metaphysical literature.

Recently this organization seems to have shifted its primary focus away from spiritual scientific research and toward being a forum for popular psychology and spirituality. It continues to publish articles related to its original purpose in a monthly email newsletter, however. Dr. Mitchell described the purpose of IONS as "learning how to take our species to the next level of its evolution."[50]

Five years after the founding of IONS, in 1976, an unusual three-volume set of books was published. Titled *A Course in Miracles*, this work was another early example of spiritual wisdom channeled by an unlikely medium. The authors, Helen Schucman and William Thetford, were Professors of Medical Psychology at Columbia University's College of Physicians and Surgeons in New York City.

Neither Schucman nor Thetford were religious or spiritual. Professor Schucman considered herself to be an atheist. When she began having highly symbolic dreams, however, and receiving unusual information while awake, Thetford encouraged her to write down the messages she received.

Dr. Schucman said she did not go into a trance, or experience automatic writing, nor did she actually hear voices. Instead, she received a sort of rapid-fire dictation which she took down in a shorthand notebook. Thetford then typed the text from her notes. The three volumes that were created in this manner became the course text, a workbook for students, and a manual for teachers. All three books have since been combined into a single volume which remains in print.[51]

A Course in Miracles is intended to help its readers advance toward spiritual enlightenment. It is as pithy as the Seth material, but more didactic. In many ways it echoes and reinforces Seth's messages, which suggests the possibility that the two works share a common source. Unlike, the Seth material, however, *A Course in Miracles* builds upon and reinforces Christian teachings and offers an excellent introduction to non-religious spirituality for readers of the Christian faith.

The *Workbook for Students* consists of 365 lessons that are designed to be done no quicker than one per day. These lessons are essential to understanding the text. The *Manual for Teachers* is presented as answers to twenty-eight hypothetical questions about the nature of life and reality. The text, workbook, and manual are available in print and digital forms, including a searchable format, from the Foundation for Inner Peace, the organization appointed by Dr. Schucman to publish and distribute the course materials.[52]

Although not formally a religious organization, a loosely connected group of followers of *A Course in Miracles* exists in locations around the world. These pilgrims get together to study and discuss the text and the lessons in hope of better understanding them.[53]

In 1980, four years after *A Course in Miracles* first came out, another seminal book, *The Aquarian Conspiracy,* was published, and quickly became a best seller.[54] This exhaustive exploration of emerging trends, compiled by writer Marilyn Ferguson, explained in everyday terms that the world was about to experience massive changes physically, spiritually, and intellectually.

With remarkable prescience, Ferguson predicted the changes we are now seeing. She defined the Aquarian Conspiracy as an army of hundreds of influential thinkers and writers throughout the world who saw changes coming. Ferguson identified dozens of authors, philosophers, and political leaders who realized that the current ways of the world were not sustainable. She said her conspiracy had no evil intent but was a harbinger of change for the better.

Many of the subjects mentioned in this book are covered in much greater depth and detail in *The Aquarian Conspiracy*. These include the Transcendentalists and the social movements of the 1960s, as well as the American Revolution and subsequent founding of the United States. Ferguson documented her theory with academic rigor, not only building a strong case for discarding the old ways, but also suggesting what a new world order might look like. *The Aquarian Conspiracy* remains in print to this day and is as appropriate now as it was when first published a generation ago.

A Spate of Spirit Channels

Jane Roberts may have been the first person in modern times to channel huge amounts of information from a spirit entity and to disseminate that information to large audiences around the world. To do this, she would go into a trance state in which her body was taken over by the spirit known as Seth. Videos of Roberts channeling Seth clearly show the changes she went through. Her eyes became darker, her mannerisms became masculine, and her voice became deeper.

Even her accent changed. Roberts' normal voice was quite nasal, with dialectic inflections characteristic of upstate New York where she lived; her Seth voice was that of an Italian immigrant—Seth's most recent incarnation on earth. The physical stress of these changes took a toll on her, however, leading to an early death at age fifty-five.

Spirit channeling has apparently become easier and less stressful in recent years, enabling hundreds of people to develop this ability, often without going into a full trance. As I will explain in coming chapters, this is part of the current shift in energy patterns in our world. Over the past forty years, many of these channelers have published transcripts of their sessions.

While the best of these channeled works have proven to be loaded with good information, others are clearly off the mark and possibly fraudulent. Some may be conveying information from forces with less than honorable intent. Because these messages are channeled through human beings, they can also be influenced and distorted by the channeler's personal attitudes and beliefs.

A peculiar aspect of these channeled works is that some of them are targeted at specific groups of individuals. If you are meant to hear or read the messages, they will find you. If, however, you never hear of a particular channel or series of books, or if you start reading but get nothing from the message, you can assume you were not yet ready or meant to receive the information.

The most reliable channeled works all say the same thing, although sometimes in different ways. They give the same reasons for historic events, offer the same explanations for current affairs, and tell of the same choices our society will face in coming years. Those that lack this consistency are suspect and may not be authentic.

There is always a possibility, of course, that channelers could be influenced by the works of other channelers that they have read or heard. Critical readers will see differences in clarity of thought, rationality of concepts, and consistency of basic tenets, that readily separates the authentic channelers from the fakes. Just as most people can discern between the truth and lies told by people they know, it is also easy to see that difference in these spiritual writings.

The most readable and easily understandable source of information on the new reality may be the series of *Conversations with God* books by Neale Donald Walsch. The first of these books was published in 1995 and quickly became a bestseller. Walsch is still writing and has nearly two dozen books, DVDs, and a movie available. He presents workshops all over the world spreading the messages received in his conversations with God.[55]

Walsch claims he never intended to be an author or a channel for spiritual messages. He was simply frustrated with the way his life was moving. To deal with his mid-life frustrations, he sat down one night and wrote out some questions to God. To his surprise, his questions were answered by way of automatic writing—a phenomenon that has been practiced by psychics and religious scholars for hundreds of years.

After writing a question, Walsch found his hand and pen writing the answers without his conscious input. The result is a library of information that answers the questions people have been asking for millennia about the nature of life, death, and reality. The information in these books makes sense, is consistent with other channeled readings, and is highly applicable to our daily lives in these chaotic times.

Kryon Arrives

The most startlingly prescient and enlightening channeled works published recently may be the Kryon sessions channeled by a mild-mannered California audio engineer named Lee Carroll. The Kryon readings have been published in more than a dozen books, which have been translated into nearly two hundred international editions, as of the time of this writing, with more promised.[56]

The first book, *The End Times*, came out in 1993 and included channeled sessions that began in 1989.[57] As its title suggests, this book provides explicit information on the changes we are experiencing today. In it, Lee Carroll describes how he reluctantly became a channel for a spirit entity known as Kryon.

Unlike Seth, Kryon never incarnated as a human on this earth. His claimed cosmic purpose is to adjust the magnetic energy of the planets to accommodate changes such as we are now experiencing. While this may sound simply too strange to accept, the unusually sharp movement of the magnetic north pole that occurred a decade ago was foretold by Kryon in his first book, which was published before the polar movement occurred.

At that time, Kryon said that he was about to adjust the earth's magnetic grid, and that the process would take twelve years, ending in 2004. He also said that the most noticeable effect of this change would be a dramatic movement of the magnetic north pole away from the polar axis of the earth. Such an astounding statement that is later proven by scientific measurement to have actually occurred, certainly adds credibility to everything else that Kryon says.

The Kryon material was at first intended only for a group of ancient souls who are now incarnate on this earth for the purpose of easing our transition into a new way of thinking and living. According to Kryon, people in this group all experienced a series of lifetimes in Lumeria, a former continent located in the middle of the Pacific Ocean, that he says sunk below the ocean but included what are now the Hawaiian Islands, some 52,000 years ago.

Kryon agrees with Seth and Michael, that we are all part of an energy entity that we call God; that we are eternal spiritual beings—he calls us angels—temporarily inhabiting human bodies; that we reincarnate many times into this earthly experience; and that we are all following paths toward enlightenment. He says that our spiritual growth has accelerated dramatically in recent decades and that many of us are ready for graduation from this learning experience.[58]

Kryon says that the early prophesies of world destruction by a giant asteroid at the turn of the millennium were correct, but that plan has changed. He confirms the claims of Metaphysicists and astrologers that the earth was tested in August 1987, a time known as the Harmonic Convergence, when all of the planets were aligned.[59] He says that the earth's population had attained a level of spiritual enlightenment at that time that cancelled the plan of destruction and let us to move into the next age.

Kryon also says that his realignment of the earth's magnetic energy grid enables us to become more enlightened more quickly; more aware of, and attuned to, the spirit world; and better able to co-create our lives with help from the spirit guides. He says the new earth energy also makes it more difficult to maintain the uncompassionate and unenlightened, fear-based attitudes and behavior that have dominated our politics, religions, and personal lives for centuries.

He further says that the magnetic realignment has triggered the climate and other changes we have been seeing in our planet. In *Kryon Book 11, Lifting the Veil*, Kryon says that this magnetic change has also made it possible for the ancient prophets to return to earth, and that they are all here now, although not in human form.[60]

Kryon says that many humans born since 1992 have DNA that is encoded to function within the new magnetic grid. He says that humans born before 1992 can change their DNA by consciously becoming more enlightened. He also says that those who cannot adapt to the changes will leave, but will come back in their next life with the new genetic alignment.

Kryon tells us that many humans are now able to use the new abilities we have been given, but have not yet realized that we can. These abilities include healing ourselves and others, making our dreams and desires come true almost immediately, and learning to communicate directly and work closely with our spirit guides.[61]

Lee Carroll has channeled Kryon in public sessions before large audiences all over the world, including seven presentations to the Society for Enlightenment and Transformation at United Nations headquarters in New York. We are now experiencing the physical disruption of our world that Kryon predicted, but are still waiting to see the positive personal and social changes. All of the Kryon books remain in print, and are now widely available to anyone concerned about the physical, spiritual, and social changes happening in our world.

The New Caretakers

Kryon tells us that there are now many advanced souls living in our midst who are here for the express purpose of preparing our world for the possibility of the change. The ancient Judaic practice of Kabala teaches that every generation includes advanced souls whose purpose is to guide society toward spiritual enlightenment.[62] Some of these advanced souls are called Indigo Children because of the unusual purple-blue color of their auras. Lee Carroll, with Jan Tober, has authored three books on Indigo Children.[63]

The Indigos are characterized by high intelligence, multiple creative talents, and a driving need to constantly improve whatever social and physical situation they find themselves in. Indigos were responsible for creating the United States government, for many of our modern inventions and social innovations, and for the now universal use of scientific inquiry.[64]

Indigo Children began arriving more frequently in the late 1930s and have been showing up in large numbers since about 1970. Indigos initiated the peace and enlightenment movement of the 1960s.

They are known for their rebellious natures, unwillingness to conform to society, and strong ethical standards.

Indigos are quick to identify liars, hypocrites, and cheats, and are not easily fooled by parents, teachers, or societal leaders. The Indigos are here to shake things up. As more Indigo Children take their places in adult society, they are leading the effort to expose fraud, hypocrisy, and unethical behavior in government, religion, and business.

Another group of these advanced beings are Transcendental Souls that have already experienced a full cycle of lives and, until recently, rarely materialized on earth at this stage of their development. They are characterized by serene wisdom and an apparent ability to perform acts of healing or magic that is unavailable to most normal people.[65]

These souls are still youngsters and are known to spiritual writers as Crystal Children.[66] Like the Indigo Children, they seem to have arrived here preprogrammed with different software—different perceptions of the world and ways of thinking—than their parents and older siblings. Some channeled works, including the Kryon readings and *A Course in Miracles*, have suggested that these individuals may be a more evolved form of human species or may be bringing life experiences from other worlds.

Crystal Children have personalities and demeanors that are different from Indigo Children. They tend to be more serene and self-assured. They often look much older than their chronological age. They are gentle, loving, and a joy to be around. These youngsters frequently come out with statements that reject the old order of society with startling clarity and wisdom. They seem to be in total control of their lives and their environments.

The recent surge in diagnoses of attention deficit disorder, autism, and Asperger's syndrome may be a result of the medical community misunderstanding Crystal Children. These youngsters simply do not conform to the expectations of our society. They appear to be distracted, bored by traditional schooling, and not interested in subjects their parents and teachers consider important.

Crystal Children often begin speaking later than normal and then speak words or whole sentences that seem to be beyond their years. Unlike actual autistics, however, Crystal Children relate well to others and do not display antisocial behavior. Some of these children are beginning to show an astounding ability to heal themselves and those around them. Their touch seems to have unusual energy and warmth. You can see this energy as light under some conditions—not unlike the healing finger of the fictional ET.[67]

Parents of Crystal Children sometimes report that their offspring seem to have an uncanny ability to communicate telepathically. This telepathic ability of the Crystal Children extends not only to humans, but also to animals, plants, rocks, and every other earthly thing. Many Crystal Children also seem to be born with knowledge of mineral crystals and how to use them to heal themselves and others.

Strangely, Crystal Children often react badly or not at all to chemical drugs. They do, however, respond well to homeopathic and herbal treatments. Some researchers have noticed subtle changes in the DNA of this new group of humans, which may explain these reactions to chemical medications.[68]

While the Indigos are here to shake up the status quo, the Crystals are the new caretakers. They have come to teach us and guide us into the new age. It appears that this new generation has arrived not only with advanced abilities that are latent in most of us, but also with implanted lessons that will be needed to adjust to the world changes that are happening now.

Crystals are leading the way quietly and without fanfare by their example. Their way of thinking and dealing with others is very different from what we are accustomed to. These children are exceptionally creative. As they mature and move into positions of authority, expect to see dramatic changes in the way people think, live, work, worship, and interact with each other.

Pepper Lewis, who channels Gaia, the spirit of our planet, has written that a new generation of humans "...that is poised to be genetically divine" began arriving in 2007.[69] Ms. Lewis says that this group will be unusually peaceful and creative, and instrumental in creating the sort of lives that we all aspire to live. She says that they will be recognizable by the "decidedly violet" color of their eyes. This group promises to be even more advanced and enlightened than the Crystal Children. Their arrival, like that of the Indigoes, is also predicted by the Kabala.

What Can We Believe?

There are, and have always been, individuals in every society that seem to possess abilities beyond what most people consider normal. These are the psychics, seers, and mediums who seem to inherently understand the nature of reality and who often can access the spiritual realm with ease for the benefit of those who cannot. They are not the charlatans who travel with carnivals and tell you that you are about to win the lottery or meet the love of your life. You know they are fakes if they ask you for information while giving a reading.

Nor are they the many amateur seers you might encounter at a psychic fair. These people may be well meaning, but they often misinterpret the messages they are receiving. You will know when you have met a genuinely gifted psychic because the information you receive will be astonishingly insightful and demonstrate a degree of knowledge that could not possibly be available to a stranger. The best psychics will not ask you to volunteer information, as it could distort their interpretation of the messages they are receiving.

I believe that now is the time to recognize these individuals as teachers and accept them into society. A few of us are beginning to realize that we all have some psychic powers; we simply have not yet learned how to use them. The Crystal Children have this knowledge and are acting as the messengers of hope to their older family members. They also seem to be introducing us to the new world order and assuring us that we need not fear the changes that we are seeing. The following paragraphs outline some of the more important points these messengers are giving us.

Our earth is alive. Our planet earth is not an inert rock hurtling through space; it is a living energy organism. It follows a precise path through the cosmos that influences all of our lives by its interaction with other galactic bodies, including our sun, our moon, and the other planets in our solar system. Our earth and every person, plant, and creature on it are the product of, and an integral part of, a universal intelligence.

We might call that universal intelligence God, Allah, All That Is, or any number of names. It exists and we are all a part of it, both individually and collectively. We all vibrate with a universal energy, as does the planet we inhabit. As each of us individually becomes more enlightened, the frequency of our vibrations increases. Collectively, we in turn increase the vibration of the planetary energy.

We are all one. Michael tells us that at some point, usually when we are two years old, we realize that we are physically independent of other beings and of the earth itself. At that time, we forget an important piece of knowledge that we brought with us when we were born. That is the knowledge that we are all connected with each other, not just in thought, but in physical energy. The spiritual readings, including Seth, Michael, and Kryon, tell us that we each split off from a common energy source and will eventually return to that source.

We are not alone. Our solar system is one of billions within the Milky Way Galaxy, and our galaxy is only one of countless numbers known and unknown. To presume that ours is the only inhabited planet may be the ultimate vanity. Surely there are other planets similar to earth, inhabited by creatures like us.

There are most certainly forms of intelligent life on planets that are different from us and our planet. Our limited means of perception and measurement simply keep us from recognizing them. Just as a radio or television must be tuned to a certain frequency in order to receive a particular program, we too are tuned to perceive a specific reality to the exclusion of all else. Despite these limitations, we may be connected to entities in other worlds in ways we cannot begin to conceptualize.

We live forever. Although our physical bodies are born to die, our fundamental selves—the persons that we are—live forever. There may have been a beginning and there may be an end to our spiritual existence, but both lie so infinitely far away as to not exist at all. Over the years, we each occupy many bodies. In between these physical lives, we continue to exist but in noncorporeal form. Swedenborg described this life between lives two hundred and fifty years ago. He wrote that we continue between lives to work, play, and interact with our friends and family, just as we do in "real" life.

During these intervals, we devote some effort to reviewing what we did right and what we did wrong in the previous lifetime. We review what we learned and we think about what we have left to learn and experience in future lives. We confer with others to decide when and where to be born again; what roles to play in the next life; and with whom we will primarily interact in that life. We choose who our parents will be; whether we will be male or female; what illnesses, handicaps, or other challenges we might decide to face; and the general outline of our next life.

While none of our lives is predestined, we do make choices between potential events and courses of action as we go along. Some of these decisions are made consciously; others are decided while we are sleeping and testing alternative realities through our dreams. This action explains those moments of déjà vu that we all experience, when we realize that we have seen a slice of life before. We saw and tried it out in our dreams.

As we progress through this endless series of lives, we may combine with other aspects of ourselves that previously lived other lives, so that we enter the next lifetime with the deep subconscious knowledge attained by the combined fragments of all our life experiences. Since time does not exist in linear fashion except in our material world, we are actually living all our lives at the same time—not just our past lives, but also our future lives. With practice, we might someday learn how to access the knowledge gained in these past and future lives for use in our current lives.

We are safe. Knowing that our essential selves never die or disappear in any other manner is the ultimate assurance that we live in a safe universe. Our physical form changes, and our environment will certainly be different, but we live forever. As this knowledge becomes more widely known and accepted within the earthly community, we might change our attitudes toward life, death, and the way we conduct our lives and relate to others. We will, in effect, become more godlike.

Our world is changing. Our earth and all its inhabitants are leaving behind an era of violence, fear, mistrust, and conflict. The old ways of thinking—fear, hatred, greed, hypocrisy, selfishness, arrogance, hubris, dishonesty, and control of others—will pass. We are about to enter an era of worldwide cooperation, compassion, and love.

We are embracing the spiritual component of reality and realizing that there is more to life than that which meets the eye. We are entering a new kind of prosperity, not one of the material things that have occupied us until now, but rather one of prosperity of human fulfillment that allows every one of us to explore and succeed in our own ways.

This is a time to celebrate; a time to release our hold on material things; and a time to embrace the spiritual and emotional connections that tie us all together. It is a time to free ourselves from the demands and control of others. Most of all, it is a time for each of us to find our calling and to follow our individual path to personal fulfillment.

The Skeptics

There are many among us who just cannot accept these ideas. That is as it should be. At some point, the skeptics will come to recognize the nature of reality; they simply are not ready yet. There are groups of people that need to get on board soon, however, or they will retard the enlightenment of everybody else. These are the leaders of our society—the people at the highest levels of government, academia, science, and religion who are in positions to influence how the rest of us think and act.

There are also many people who simply mistrust everybody and every idea. These folk seldom occupy positions of authority, but they often can influence the attitudes of similarly disenfranchised people who think as they do. These suspicious skeptics now have an open channel of communication, thanks to the Internet and the proliferation of sociopathic talk-radio and television personalities who constantly stir up fear, hatred, and bigotry.

It seems to be a law of life that a small group of any population mistrusts everybody else and suspects that others are conspiring against their interests. These people seem to especially mistrust government, and often with good reason. They see the bungling mismanagement and difficulty of getting anything productive done in a political environment as signs of evil conspiracies within government.

More enlightened thinkers realize that government mismanagement and unproductive behavior are not signs of conspiracy but more often the result of lack of cooperation among political leaders. This fact of political life by itself argues against the possibility of conspiracy. To be successful, any conspiracy requires complete cooperation, agreement, secrecy, and commitment among its players. None of these traits is commonly found in government.

Government leaders are all politicians by necessity, and politicians rely for their survival on tradition and situations that do not change or that evolve slowly over long periods of time. Change frightens them and threatens their positions. They may campaign on promises to change things, but once in power, they will do everything possible to protect the status quo.

The new communications tools, combined with the no-nonsense attitude of the generation of Indigos and Crystals now coming into positions of authority, are making government much more open and democratic than ever before. It is already becoming very difficult for authoritarian leaders to survive. The old systems are collapsing of their own weight soon to be replaced by more enlightened thoughts and action.

Scientists tend to be skeptical too. By their own definition, they accept as reality only that which they can repeatedly identify, measure, quantify, and define. While we might expect them to take an agnostic approach to anything that they do not fully understand, withholding judgment until further evidence is found, scientists in all fields more often deny the validity or existence of anything that has not been scientifically proven.

It is through science that we will solve the problems of energy shortages, disease, and climate changes. Before any of this can happen, though, we need to change our thinking about the traditional scientific approach. Modern scientists are beginning to take off their blinders and open their minds to the complex interconnections of our reality and realize that their measuring instruments and techniques are limited, and that there is much that they do not know.

We think of the art of healing as a science and the science of astrology as a trivial pastime. We have much yet to learn about both. Healing will improve when we stop thinking of the body as a mechanical device to be treated solely with chemical drugs and physical operations and recognize the powers of the mind and soul to cure bodily imbalances. According to *A Course in Miracles*, illness is an illusion that is chosen in a misguided effort to solve other problems in one's life.[70]

We also need to reconsider the ancient science of astrology and realize that it would not have endured for so many thousands of years if it did not have a legitimate basis and be of value to society. As our scientists learn more about the importance of the earth's magnetic field to our survival and the ways it influences our physical bodies, they may also discover the basis of how astrology works and the importance of astrological effects on our lives.

Perhaps nothing in our society changes more slowly than religious thought and doctrine. Clinging as they do to ancient texts and creeds, the established religions can take centuries to adjust to societal changes. Religious leaders no longer control the lives and minds of broad populations in enlightened societies, although they remain strong in more primitive nations and in rural areas of the United States.

Even in the Bible belt, however, attitudes are now changing. Young evangelical Christians, for instance, tend to be more focused on issues of social justice than on the issues of personal morality and control of other people's behavior that dominate the beliefs of their parents and grandparents.

Public opinion pollsters such as the Pew Forum on Religion and Public Life have found an abrupt shift in answers to their questions on religious affiliation. They are frequently hearing respondents describe themselves as "spiritual but not religious."

As more and more people move away from traditional religious beliefs, the established churches will continue to lose influence. This does not mean an end to spiritual beliefs, though. As adherents move away from the controlling and fear-based dogma of the old religions, they might eventually return to the love-based teachings upon which all religions were originally founded.

Testing for Truth

It can be hard to tell truth from fiction when you look for information on the 2012 shift. As new information sources began to emerge in the 1970s, a spate of false sources also appeared. Copycat authors, looking to cash in on a popular craze, and probably not recognizing the real source of the spiritual texts, published countless books and articles claiming to predict and explain future events. Even some well-respected channelers have produced work that conflicts with accepted doctrine. Often this is a result of misinterpreting long-range predictions as being imminent.

Fictional works based upon spiritual truths have also become popular in recent years. The number of television shows, movies, and novels with such themes has burgeoned and been widely accepted by a population that is searching for answers to questions that are not being addressed by science, government, or religion.

Novels such as *The Celestine Prophecy* and *The Da Vinci Code* make no pretense of being anything but fiction. While they have proven to be wildly popular and entertaining, they should not be confused with books that are carrying new truths from the spiritual realm. This trend in popular spirituality also confirms that many of us sense the magnitude of the changes that we are seeing and want to learn more about them.

How do you tell authentic texts from the bogus? Old time journalists looked for "the truth cooked three ways." A three-part test works well in this case too. Ask yourself these three sets of questions when gauging the authenticity of what you are reading or hearing:

> Does what you are reading or hearing make sense to you? Is it reasonable? Does it square with your personal experiences and observations of the world that you know?
>
> Is this text or message consistent with other texts and messages and with the teachings of known and respected Metaphysicists and authors that you have come to trust?
>
> Have any of the predictions made in these texts or messages been verified by scientific observation, measurement, or tests?

You will find that the readings suggested here all meet these tests with startling regularity. There are other authentic texts that have been channeled by mediums not mentioned here that also meet these tests. Read and decide for yourself. If you find that you simply cannot accept the admittedly unorthodox concepts presented here, try to keep an open mind to the possibility that they might have merit and that they only present a different way of looking at the world.

PART IV – WHAT TO EXPECT

<u>A Wild Ride Ahead</u>

The new age on the horizon promises to be a positive one, with its visions of a more enlightened population bringing us worldwide peace, equality, cooperation, compassion, and personal fulfillment. The adjustment has been rough, though, and it is likely to get worse before we begin to see lasting effects of the positive changes. The past decade has been a hard one for all of us; the next decade could be even tougher.

The Internal Displacement Monitoring Centre in Oslo, Norway, estimated that forty-two million persons were displaced from their homes by natural disasters in 2010 alone. The United Nations High Commissioner for Refugees, Antonio Guterres, speaking at a conference on climate change in Oslo in June 2011, said:

> "There is increasing evidence to suggest that natural disasters are growing in frequency and intensity and that this is linked to the longer-term process of climate change."[71]

Meteorologists are already predicting that the unusually fierce hurricanes, typhoons, tornados, and other severe storms that we have been experiencing recently could be the new normal, representing a trend that will bring us even more devastating weather in the near future. They tell us that more temperate regions can expect to continue seeing harsher winters and scorching summers, and that polar regions will continue to thaw, causing sea levels to rise even further.

Both Kryon and Michael predict that the population of the earth could be reduced by as much as five percent during this shift. That might not seem like a huge number, but consider that five percent of the current world population, for example, is almost exactly equal to the total population of the United States.

Many of these deaths would result from natural calamities, wars, political genocide, and starvation in regions of the world that are ill prepared to deal with the changes. We have already seen this happening in Rwanda, Iraq, Indonesia, India, Myanmar, and Haiti.

In more advanced societies we are likely to see more people succumbing to early departure from diseases and violence related to the stress and frustration of the climactic, economic, and societal changes. These are not bold predictions; they are simply recognition of what is already happening in our over-stressed and fear-filled world.

The worldwide economic upheaval of 2008 may have been merely a warning shot of even more dire financial difficulties to come. Some economists are now predicting that we could see a complete collapse of the world's economy if strong actions are not taken immediately to change the fundamental way we do business and measure success.

For the past two centuries the developed world has maintained an economy based almost solely upon the exploitation of natural resources and constant economic growth. We have been living in a world dependent upon ever-increasing manufacturing, processing, transporting, selling, and consuming of hard and soft goods and materials. Economists and clear-thinking people have long known that this sort of economy is not sustainable indefinitely. Few expected it to end so abruptly, however.

During the last century, a worldwide financial industry has been built upon the illusion that money has value in itself, and can be bought, sold, and manipulated just as are resources and hard goods. The world is beginning to realize that the creation and trading of stocks, bonds, commodity futures, insurance, mortgages and other loans, and all of the various derivatives that have evolved from such paper assets, has no fundamental basis in reality. It is simply a game that transfers wealth from the many to the few.

As the stars in this game have continued to concentrate wealth among fewer individuals, the working people who create real worth in society have been squeezed out of jobs, savings, and opportunities to the point where many can no longer afford to buy the hard goods or borrow the money that kept the process working.

Our planet is now in the process of closing down a system that we have not controlled ourselves. Consumerism is dying. It may be resuscitated in the short term, with much help from consumers in China, India, and the African countries whose economies will be expanding over the next few decades, but it cannot survive in the long term. Adjusting to a completely different economic system could take several generations. In the meantime, expect to see lasting unemployment, underemployment, and financial stress as we continue to lose assets and learn to support ourselves in new and unconventional ways.

Government reaction to these events is not likely to be effective and could make things even worse. If they take action at all, political leaders are likely to try stimulating growth, promoting consumerism, or falling back on similar strategies that have been used in the past, not realizing that these actions will not be as effective in the new energy as they once were. The lack of positive actions could result in the collapse of some of the world's most prominent and powerful governments.

Despite their currently competent leadership, the United States, United Kingdom, Germany, France and several other European countries are now seeing grass-roots movements that are forcing governments to be more fiscally conservative—exactly the opposite of the direction they need to move to adjust to the new energy.

Political conservatism is fear-based. It leads governments to be protectionist, isolationist, and defensive. These policies are all representative of the failed systems that are now being closed down. Our leaders need to be more inclusive, cooperative, accepting, and flexible, but none of these are traits normally associated with government.

Keep an eye on the five major trends described in Part II of this book. Watch as the rise in personal independence brings down tyrannical governments and triggers rebellions by suppressed people against any form of control by political and religious leaders. Enjoy the revelation of secrets and continue to demand integrity in business, government, religious, and personal affairs.

Notice the gradual move from competition to cooperation in all areas of life. Embrace the emerging balance between masculine belligerence and feminine compassion. Watch for the rise of a society motivated more by compassion than by fear. Most of all, learn to accept the fundamental change in attitudes shown by the young people now rising to prominence, for it portends the nature of the society that is now emerging.

The immediate future might seem bleak, but it is not hopeless and most of us will survive the adjustments. We have to understand, however, that what's happening is beyond our control, and that we must adjust to the new world order. Every one of us chose to be here to experience this great shift. We knew it would not be easy, but it will be an experience that will change us for all of eternity.

Weather Woes

It is now clear that political leaders worldwide have neither the ability nor the intent to address the inevitable effects of climate changes. It is possible that no action they could take would have any effect, even if they finally decided to do something about the climate.

The climate changes we are now experiencing may have been caused by the alteration of the planet's magnetic grid alignment, or they might be part of a normal long-term earth weather cycle. While the widespread use of fossil fuels and the destruction of tropical rain forests appear to have contributed to global warming and exacerbated the problems, these man-made activities might not have been the fundamental cause of the climate changes.

A phenomenon known as the Milankovitch theory postulates that the earth's orbit around the sun is not uniform, and that changes in the orbit create slight changes in the tilt of the earth respective to the sun. When the earth's tilt increases, summers become warmer, winters become colder, and polar ice caps partially melt.[72]

As the melted ice flows into the oceans it spreads and shifts the weight distribution of water on the planet. This weight shift in turn puts excess strain on tectonic plates, with a subsequent increase in earthquakes, volcanic activity, and tsunamis.

Climate change is causing vast areas of the world to experience crop failures, with resulting famine and political unrest. Arid regions of Africa have seen mass out-migrations of refugees that strain the resources of more temperate areas that are still able to produce crops and graze animals. We could see similar outmigration in other regions.

The earthquakes, tsunamis, volcanic eruptions, and other plate tectonic events should gradually subside as the earth works through this readjustment period. Erratic temperature changes and violent windstorms could continue well beyond our lifetimes, however. Residents of vulnerable regions might be wise to consider moving to safer places.

As odd and counter-intuitive as it seems, the global warming we are now experiencing could actually be a precursor of a coming ice age. Another indicator of an imminent ice age is the reduction in the strength of the planet's magnetic field, an effect that earth scientists have learned from analysis of core samples taken from iron-bearing soils. Kryon tells us there will be a mini ice age similar to the one experienced 600 years ago that covered northern Europe with glaciers, but that it will not occur for another 300 years.[73]

Rather than trying to stop, alter, or reverse global warming and other symptoms of climate change, our political leaders and earth scientists would be far more productive if they focus instead on ways that we might alter our behavior to adapt to the changes. It is not too soon to begin planning to relocate residents of low-lying Pacific islands and coastal areas that are already experiencing unprecedented periodic flooding and could soon be completely inundated.

The United States government began regulating coastal development nearly forty years ago, and has recently updated its flood insurance maps to reflect higher average sea levels and storm surges.

Building codes throughout the world's developed countries are being stiffened to reduce potential damage from earthquakes and high winds. And new awareness of the destructive power of water has come from the increased frequency and force of tsunami activity.

News reports on climate change tend to focus on its adverse effects, or on the statements of clueless preachers or politicians denying its reality. There could be benefits, though, that result from the climate change, including the opening of northern ocean shipping routes through areas that were previously covered with ice year-round; access to petroleum and natural gas that is now inaccessible under the polar ice caps; and the discovery of previously unknown natural resources in these areas.

Parts of Canada, Russia, Greenland, and other areas that have been too frigid for agriculture, or even for normal habitation, might someday become temperate enough to be farmed to counter the loss of arable land in more arid regions. More visionary and entrepreneurial businesses could profit from the effects of climate change, while those who are mired in the old ways of thinking and doing business are likely to falter.

The New World Economy

Economic growth since the beginning of the industrial revolution that began more than 200 years ago has been driven primarily by two factors: constant increase in population and a steady rise in personal standards of living. Both of these factors are now changing. The rate of population growth has slowed dramatically over the past two decades, and could begin to decline within the next decade.

Most of the highly developed Western and European countries are even now shrinking or growing only through immigration from less civilized areas. China's policy of limiting families to one child will continue to affect its population growth for many years. As primitive cultures become more enlightened, they are likely to trend to smaller family size.

Global growth in standard of living could initially accelerate as underdeveloped areas of Africa, Asia, Indonesia, and South and Central America seek economic parity with Europe and North America. While it took more than 200 years for the leading economic nations to reach their current levels of prosperity, the growth in the remainder of the world might take only a few decades. At that point we should see a new economic model take effect that is based not on constant growth but on sustainable wealth through individual initiative and service to others, rather than on exploitation of resources and production of hard goods.

China and India are well on the way to reaching parity with more advanced economies. Both countries hold the potential to become major world economic powers once they overcome internal political structures that are retarding their growth. China needs to depose the Baby Souls who are now in control and India needs to retire its legendarily corrupt and inefficient bureaucracy.

The Chinese are already investing heavily in Africa, recognizing that the continent abounds in natural resources and is about to blossom into what could soon become the world's strongest economy. Kryon tells us the African nations could soon unite into a single country, based on the political model of the United States, and become a dominant force in the world economy within the lifetime of many of us.[74]

A New Way of Working

A primary trait of this world's culture for the past two millennia has been the need to work hard not just for our own sakes, but so that others might profit. Work has almost universally meant toil, drudgery, boredom, and often danger, in order to survive to work some more. This pattern is now changing.

The new generation coming into power no longer lives to work but works to live. These bright and ambitious workers are less motivated by money and more in doing work that uses their natural talents, benefits others, and is personally rewarding.

That does not mean these workers are lazy or unproductive. On the contrary, when work is rewarding and fun, people can be exceedingly productive. When you work for money, you do what is required; when you love your work, you will constantly think of new ways to do it better.

This change of individual attitudes comes at a time when societal attitudes toward work also need to change. The Puritan work ethic that demands forty hours a week or more of intense labor in order to reach a basic standard of living is clearly obsolete. Business owners and their financial backers have continued to promote hard work as a moral virtue in order to squeeze more productivity and profit out of those who are producing their wealth.

Those at the top rarely work hard themselves, but create their wealth from harnessing the work of others. A notable exception can be found in the entrepreneurs who create new endeavors, and may be the hardest workers of all. They are not working from some mythical moral imperative or desire for money, though, but from the pure joy of creation and success.

The world now has far more people available to work than there is work to do. As we move away from a consumer society that is based upon the exploitation of people and resources, the problem of unemployment is likely to become even worse.

We need to rework our economic system so that more people work fewer hours to maintain a basic standard of living. Those who want to work longer or smarter should benefit from their contributions. Those who work only to survive should be free to devote their efforts elsewhere, including important but poorly paid work such as child or elder care.

This is not an impossible dream. With our instant communications and automated factories, fewer people are needed to produce and distribute the goods we desire. Despite enormous productivity gains from the introduction of computer technology and self-service conveniences, there remains plenty of room for further improvements.

The benefits of past productivity gains have gone primarily to investors and corporate executives, with limited price reductions passed on to consumers. Workers, however, have not been rewarded. Their jobs have often been eliminated or outsourced to third-world countries. As productivity has improved, workers who have not been laid off have seen their benefits reduced and their workloads increased.

The opportunities for positive changes in the way we work are unlimited. If we shift things around so that more of us live near where we work and work near where we live, we would be able to produce more work while having more time to live. This is a change that can happen slowly over time with no extra investment needed by either private business or government.

Think of the number of wasted hours that would be freed up if we eliminated the need for a daily commute, or even reduced it by half. This one change alone would save many billions of dollars in fuel use, vehicle wear, road maintenance, day care, and stress-related medical care, not to mention the positive effects on air and water quality and conservation of natural resources.

We live in dwellings that are empty most of the day, while working in shops and offices that are unused much of the time. Why should so many workers have to waste an hour or more every workday in order to sit in a cubicle with a computer and telephone, when they could do the same work from home or from shared office space in their home neighborhood?

We should not abandon the suburbs nor move to the cities, as some futurists have suggested, but we should instead focus on the neighborhoods of each, making them all places where we can live, work, and play without wasting hours every day moving between these pursuits.

One might argue that we cannot mix residential neighborhoods with heavy industrial plants such as steel mills, foundries, and refineries the way we did a century ago. Back then these industries employed thousands of workers and severely polluted the ground, air, and water where workers lived.

The same industries now are so fully automated that they employ only a small fraction of the number of workers they once needed. They require higher levels of education and expertise from those they do employ, which also raises the economic standards of those employees. Most importantly, today's factories do not pollute the way their predecessors did. The time may have come to reconsider the concept of company towns, where employees live only a short walk from the factories, shops, and offices where they work.

Redefining Wealth

This planet holds all the resources necessary to provide abundant food, shelter, education, and personal fulfillment for everyone. Distribution of these resources has been inequitable throughout history, however. As we move into a new age, we are likely to come up against new challenges and discover new opportunities, but everybody can have the basic resources they need to prosper. With a slightly smaller population, new political and economic systems, and more equitable distribution of wealth, our earth can provide adequate food, housing, and protection for everyone.

To fully comprehend this new concept of abundance, we need to better understand the difference between having wealth and being rich, as well as the difference between lacking money and being poor. Many people lack money but lead rich lives and are not poor in any way other than the lack of material goods. Others have plenty of money and more things than they can ever enjoy but lead empty lives that are not rich by any standard.

Wealth and poverty have more to do with attitudes and expectations than with any accounting of material resources. The poor person will whine that his life circumstances are someone else's fault and complain that nobody is doing anything to help. The person who is financially broke but not poor will take responsibility for his position, regardless of its cause, and look for ways to work out of it.

Even during the Great Depression of the 1930s, a few people became fabulously wealthy by refusing to let the prevailing attitude of poverty defeat them. Howard Hughes, Walt Disney, and Henry Ford, for example, became extraordinarily wealthy and successful by relying on their talents and resources and looking for opportunities to satisfy the needs of others while doing what they enjoyed.

In the new world order, material goods might be far less abundant, but they could also be far less desired, than they are now. We should not see this as a hardship. We might find that we are relieved not to be burdened by the costs and time required to maintain our material things. As we move away from Young Soul thinking toward Mature Soul values, abundance is more likely to be measured not in material assets, but in health, happiness, personal satisfaction, and new opportunities to contribute to society.

Direct Communications

Newspapers have long prided themselves for being the watchdogs of government through investigative reporting and public exposure of unethical or illegal behavior. As print papers disappear, their advocates have predicted that there will no longer be anyone watching over government.

The opposite is closer to what is now happening, however. In the past, the only access the electorate had within the halls of government was through the newspapers. Now we all not only have instant access via the Internet, but we also have the ability to instantly register our opposition or support of government activities.

The rise of personal free will and the loss of ability to manipulate and control others is changing the way that people relate to each other at all levels. We are now less likely to hold on to a restrictive or abusive personal relationship than previous generations were. That applies not just to mates and partners, but also to jobs, communities, religions, organizations, and friendships.

Changes in communications have dramatically altered the way we relate to friends and family. We used to make most of our personal and business connections face to face or by letter. The telegraph and telephone allowed us to communicate instantly at a distance. Now most of our communications are electronic and instantaneous, with people in the same neighborhood, the same household, the same building, or even the same room.

These changes in the ways we communicate may seem to make our relationships less personal, but they have also greatly expanded the frequency and range of our connections, and the number of people with whom we have daily contact. Whether you see these changes as for better or for worse, they most certainly have altered the way we live and relate to each other. In many ways, we have become closer to each other and yet more individual and independent in our actions and activities. This is the new model for personal and business relationships.

The End of War

We may have already seen the end of war between nations. Tribal warfare within nations is likely to continue for a while, though. The political instabilities in Iraq, Iran, Afghanistan, Pakistan, China, and the entire continent of Africa are all based on ancient conflicts between competing religious sects or tribal clans. These are nations dominated by Infant and Baby Souls. As the inhabitants of these areas mature spiritually and become more enlightened, their primitive beliefs and behaviors will gradually fade.

In the meantime, droughts and loss of arable farmland that result from climate change are likely to aggravate tribal tensions. We now know from expensive experience that these conflicts cannot be settled by outside forces or political intervention by Western governments. We need to learn that they can only be resolved by the participating groups, and often only after more bloodshed and suffering.

Terrorism has become the most frightening form of warfare, as we have not figured out how to combat it. Traditional military action not only does not work against terrorism, it tends to encourage and abet its spread. International leaders seem to be at a loss as to how to do anything about terrorists. Clearly, a new approach to this problem is needed.

Evidence is building that extreme poverty and feelings of personal helplessness lie at the root of the frustration and anger that leads individuals to become involved with terrorist groups and activities. Once we begin to understand the motivation behind the behavior and deal with the root causes instead of the symptoms, we may begin to see the problem abate.

Osama Bin Laden, the purported king of the terrorists, said that his intent in engineering the attacks of September 11, 2001 was to bankrupt the United States. He nearly succeeded. He knew that the administration then in office would react exactly as it did, by ramping up expensive and ineffective military campaigns that the country could not afford. He also knew that such a reaction would become his most powerful recruiting tool for expansion of al-Qaida.

We may someday see the abandonment of military force. Our problems are no longer national; they are now global, and so is our ability to solve them. We now know how to identify the root causes of conflicts and deal with them as we move from a culture of fear to one of reason.

The majority of people of this world want peace, and they want it now, but peace cannot be attained through violent means. Leaders who fail to understand this shift are being deposed, while those who embrace the new world order are rising to positions of power, not only in free societies, but also in those with totalitarian governments.

The 2009 elections in Iran, for instance, exposed widespread dissatisfaction among the electorate with the theocracy in power and produced a strong showing by an academic who espoused democratic principles and had the backing of a majority of younger voters. The current Iranian government cannot survive in the new world energy.

The single most effective strategy used by the United States to ease the Iraq conflict was paying the insurgents to police their own neighborhoods. This may become the prototype for solution of tribal conflicts elsewhere. The ultimate key to defeating terrorists and radical insurgencies may be the global elimination of poverty and inequality that leaves too many people with no hope for living satisfying lives.

As the military forces move away from traditional warfare and become more involved in training, in peacekeeping, and in rebuilding local roads, hospitals, schools, utilities, and other resources, their training needs to take a major shift in direction.

The United States Military Academy at West Point has recently revamped its curriculum and basic teaching philosophy to accommodate changes in how wars are now evolving. Until recently, the Academy relied on rote memorization of engineering and math, along with military history. Cadets were taught to be obedient; independent thinking was discouraged. West Point is now teaching cadets to think on their feet so as to be better able to lead their troops on complex battlegrounds.[75]

Emphasis has moved away from rote learning and moved toward understanding the political and cultural issues that separate the sides of the conflict. Cadets now learn to think unconventionally in order to better deal with unconventional warfare. They are being educated rather than trained; learning foreign languages and developing the ability to reason through complex situations.

The U.S. Army is training its enlisted troops differently too. At camps set up on several bases around the country, soldiers are now working in makeshift village settings, created to simulate Middle Eastern neighborhoods. In these camps, they reenact actual incidents that occurred in Iraq or Afghanistan.

Interestingly, these policy changes are an example of the influence of feminine thinking on government policy, as they were devised by Michelle Flournoy, the first woman to move into the highest echelon of the Pentagon as Undersecretary of Defense for Policy. Ms. Flournoy is a prime example of the new energy that is bringing women into parity with men in positions of authority that have traditionally been held exclusively by males.[76]

The Evolution of Government

While the changes in our work, communications, economies, and attitudes toward war evolve over the next few generations, we might expect to see the role of government changing from historic patterns of defense and regulation into resources for growth and enlightenment.

The closer we move toward a more peaceful world, the more governments will be able to shift their priorities away from defense and into social programs. Fewer government resources will be needed for military purposes, as mutual cooperation and diplomacy replace mistrust and belligerence in intergovernmental affairs.

The meltdown of the world's financial system in 2008, triggered by unethical policies and practices of money managers in the United States, dramatically demonstrated how interdependent all nations of the world have become. In coming years we might expect this interdependency to increase and expand into areas beyond economic affairs and mutual defense and into areas of social welfare and personal freedom.

The current struggle between liberal and conservative political wings in the United States, United Kingdom, and several European countries could end up destroying the traditional system of political parties. Future leaders might hold all of the values that we now associate with disparate political philosophies. They may have little choice but to be fiscally conservative while being pressured to be socially liberal by an electorate that continues to struggle to maintain a basic standard of living in a changing world.

We might expect governments in the future to be both libertarian and socialist. They might be less involved in regulating and controlling the behavior of their constituents, of businesses, and of other governments, and more involved in providing the means and services needed for every person to live at a comfortable standard of health, safety, and personal satisfaction. The result could be the elimination of poverty and starvation, with related steep declines in crime, stress, illness, terrorism, domestic violence, and infant mortality. Freedom does not come from less government; it comes from less suffering. True freedom is freedom from fear.

As secrets are exposed in business and in personal affairs, government too is finding it more difficult to keep activities from public view. Government agencies and officials at all levels are being forced to be more open with their constituents and are subject to considerably more public scrutiny than ever before. As the general population becomes more enlightened, it is becoming increasingly difficult for government leaders to hide incompetence, malfeasance, and immorality. While it may seem that such problems are more common lately, it is because they are being more frequently exposed.

Issues of war and peace have always been the work of governments, but this too is changing. As the nature of war shifts away from conflicts between countries and increasingly involves acts of terrorism or tribal genocide, expect the peace builders to emerge outside of government in the privately funded and grass-roots organizations.

At the same time, we might see the role of the military move from one of killing and destruction to one of training and peacemaking. Astute leaders of rebellions are learning that capturing the support of the population by providing protective and social services that are not being adequately addressed by government is an effective method of overthrowing that government. One notable example of this effect is the 2007 election of Hamas in the Gaza region of the Palestinian Territories, which caught Western leaders completely by surprise. The Muslim Brotherhood is gaining support in Egypt by providing social services to the poor that are not being provided by the military government.

The structures and attitudes of government are already changing. Totalitarian regimes are toppling or struggling to survive, challenged not by outside enemies or other regimes, but by their own constituents. Democracy appears to be thriving even as increasing numbers of people begin to question the wisdom of majority rule. Conservative thinking, widely considered to be a virtue throughout most of recent history, increasingly appears to be disastrously unenlightened.

Where are these trends leading us? Government will change as the attitudes of its constituents change. As more and more people become enlightened, they will gradually abandon their fears and conduct their personal lives in a more compassionate way. Governments, like their constituents, will also become less competitive and more compassionate. They may even move away from only benefitting the wealthy and powerful and move toward providing an improved standard of living for all.

As the world's population becomes more enlightened and the average soul age advances, we are more likely to look at the governments of countries like the Netherlands, with its highly socialized services and limited controls on personal behavior, as models for the future. We will also see a rapid increase in governments cooperating—or even combining—with former enemies. Watch for the emergence of new countries formed by the combination of smaller nations in Africa, South and Central America, and Asia.

Science Opens Its Eyes

Now that we are beginning to step away from a world dominated by a focus on fear and the acquisition of material goods into a world of spiritual and intellectual enlightenment, we need to increasingly rely on the scientific community to solve our common problems. Ironically, the same scientific community that we need to lead us in new directions is also apt to lead the effort to thwart innovation and change.

As modern scientific practice developed, it became deeply entrenched in academia and fragmented into many distinct fields that often conflict and compete with each other. The various scientific disciplines have become notorious for not working together or sharing ideas. Science is too often notable for what it does not know, rather than for what it thinks it has learned.

Modern scientific inquiry first emerged at the end of the dark ages five hundred years ago, and blossomed during the ensuing renaissance period. The earliest scientists were also prominent artists, known as much for their creative abilities as for their intellectual brilliance. Leonardo da Vinci, Michelangelo Simoni, and Nicolaus Copernicus defined the practice of science as observation, experimental investigation, and theoretical explanation.

These early scientists were generally not rewarded in their own time. Although they frequently credited spiritual sources for their ideas, they were castigated by the religious establishment of the time, which felt threatened by scientific evidence that ran counter to church teachings. Copernicus, for example, realized that the earth was not the center of the universe but merely another planet that rotated around the sun. He kept this concept to himself until late in his life, however, and was considered a heretic by church leaders for this belief, which conflicted with their dogma.

Isaac Newton set the standard for modern science with the publication in 1687 of his seminal work, *Philosophiae Naturalis Principia Mathematica*. In this text, Newton drew the universe as a precise mechanical system in which everything moved with mathematically predictable certainty. He even described the nature and behavior of atoms, which he called *mass points*. Newtonian physics was universally accepted until Albert Einstein published his theory of relativity in 1906.

Researchers in the late 1800s succeeded in splitting the atom, opening up a completely new world of theoretical physics that Einstein, with help from his wife, Marić, began to explore. The Einsteins discovered the connection between mass and energy at the atomic level. They also examined the concept of time and postulated that time was not fixed, but highly elastic, changing with the speed of an object in space. Einstein's theory of relativity says that nothing can travel faster than the speed of light, about 186,000 feet per second, a standard that may have been proven false by more recent discoveries.

Startling revelations have come out over the past seventy years, primarily from scientists who specialize in the study of subatomic particles, known as quantum physics, as well as those in astronomy and microbiology. In one of Jane Roberts' books, Seth notes that "Einstein nudged time and felt it move." Modern cosmologists are nudging reality and finding it isn't there. They now realize that the minute particles of mass/energy that make up atoms do not follow the rules laid out by either Newton or Einstein. Some experiments have shown that they do not seem to follow any rules at all.

Subatomic particles apparently take whatever form they choose only when they are being watched, and even then they take one of several forms or switch instantly between forms. They also are apparently able to communicate with each other instantly and over great distances. We do not know how this happens, but it appears to be a form of energy similar to our own thoughts. At least two independent experiments have measured the speed of this "thought energy" at twenty thousand times the speed of light.[77]

Why is this concept important to the explanation of what's happening in our world? It is important because it bridges the enormous gap between science and spirituality, and opens the door to rational scientific explanation of many phenomena that we have been hearing all along from the spirit world and from the most talented Metaphysicists. The key to this explanation can be summed up in one word: coherence.

Quantum physics is showing us that our universe and everything in it is composed of various forms of energy that is completely coherent—constantly and instantaneously interconnected at its most elemental level. It is also showing us that our reality is whatever we expect it to be. Even more startling is to read of highly regarded cosmologists suggesting that our reality might be only one of billions of possible realities all existing at the same time and in the same place.[78]

What can we expect from the scientific community in coming decades? As the new generation of Indigo and Crystal Children infiltrates our scientific laboratories, attitudes will gradually change. Look for scientists to once again embrace philosophy and art in their search for creative answers to the world's problems. They are more likely to follow the advice of former astronaut and IONS founder Edgar Mitchell, who said:

> "Now is the time to develop our nonrational abilities into a 'subjective technology' which will begin the wedding of science and religion, reason and intuition, the physical and the spiritual."[79]

As advanced as our computer technology appears to be, for instance, this science is still in its early infancy compared to its ultimate potential. In the future, we should expect to see radical changes in the fundamental technology, possibly moving from silicon-based electronics to a biological base not unlike that of our own brains.

The scientific community needs to stop protecting the privacy of its specific research endeavors, and to start working across disciplines to address the complex issues now facing our world.

WHAT'S HAPPENING

Rethinking Energy

Our current use of resource-based energy, including coal, oil, gas, and atomic isotopes, will soon need to be replaced by more sustainable sources. While solar, wind, and waterpower might carry some of the burden during the transition, the biggest changes may come from steep reductions in use of power through drastic improvements in efficiency.

One of the most common wastes of energy under the current system is electric power that is lost during transmission between central generating plants and users in outlying locations. While urban centers are best served by central facilities, advances in on-site electric generation from photovoltaic panels and small wind turbines show promise for eventual replacement of hard-wired utility grids in sparsely populated areas.

As the cost of these on-site generating systems comes down, and the cost of central generation goes up, individual off-grid power supplies could become the norm for non-urban areas. At some point, neighborhood solar or wind systems might someday power even suburban neighborhoods more efficiently than wires from a central plant.

Nuclear power seemed headed for a revival until the meltdown of the Japanese plants following the

2011 tsunami. Although the gas-cooled nuclear plants used in Europe, and newer designs for water-cooled plants, are far safer than the early designs that failed in Japan, popular opinion may prevent any more nuclear generators from being built anywhere other than China and India. These rapidly- growing countries are playing economic catch-up with the West, and neither their governments nor their populace have embraced concepts of environmental protection.

Spent fuel from existing plants will continue to cause a problem, as long as our scientists and engineers assume that there is no way to deactivate it and continue to insist that it must simply be buried. Once they open their minds and begin searching beyond their limited perception, they may discover a simple and currently existing biological treatment that will deactivate the waste.

Kryon has warned us to "get cheap energy and get it soon." He suggests two largely untapped energy sources that are not only unlimited but constant and steady. These are geothermal heat from beneath the surface of the earth and tidal movement of the oceans. Both can be tapped with existing technology and at relatively little cost compared to nuclear power.[80] At some point, our scientists may even learn to harness and use the power contained within the earth's magnetic grid.[81]

A Fresh Look at Food

Climate changes are causing severe droughts in areas such as Russia, central Africa, and Australia that have been traditional sources of crops and animals raised for food. This trend is likely to spread to other regions and is resulting in scarcity of certain basic foods such as wheat and rice, with consequent increases in prices. While genetic engineering and other artificial methods of increasing production are helping to offset this scarcity, some regions of the world are already experiencing devastating famines.

We may in the future have to adjust the amounts and the kinds of food that we eat, consuming less factory-prepared food, and growing more of our own, even if it is just a tray of lettuce on a windowsill. As we adapt to the new reality, we might also find that we can maintain our weight and our energy on far less food than we have grown accustomed to eating. While this sounds ominous, a restricted diet is known to increase life expectancy and reduce illnesses related to obesity.

Humans are omnivores. We can survive on nearly every kind of food from every imaginable source, whether it is animals, poultry, seafood, fruits, vegetables, insects, or grasses. While some people, including medical and dietary specialists, advocate eating certain foods and avoiding others, we retain the innate ability to process food from any source.

When we develop allergies or other illnesses from food, the reason may have more to do with how the food is prepared than with the basic source or type of food. Ancient Jewish law spelled out in detail how animals were to be slaughtered and how food was to be prepared in a way that minimized these adverse effects. We might be wise to adhere more closely to those laws today.

Food that is processed in factories for mass consumption typically contains excessive amounts of trans-fats, sugars, salt, and chemical preservatives that interfere with normal digestion, metabolism, and other bodily processes. Some nutritionists are beginning to realize that meat, eggs, and dairy products that come from birds and animals that are kept tightly penned, overstuffed with feed that is enhanced with chemicals and hormones, and then brutally slaughtered, are not healthy for human consumption.

The same products derived from animals that are allowed to graze freely, fed natural, unenhanced feed, and honored with humane treatment at the time of slaughter, are far more beneficial for us and less likely to cause adverse reactions.[82]

For more than forty years the Western medical community has consistently advocated diets low in all forms of fat. Younger practitioners are now learning that the science behind this advice is shaky at best and has never been conclusively proven. Some are beginning to realize that a low-fat diet can actually lead to increased rates of heart disease, obesity, osteoporosis, eye problems, and some forms of cancer.

The conflict arises from the mistaken idea that the fat and cholesterol in our blood and around our bellies is the same as the fat and cholesterol that we consume in our food. We are now learning that the unhealthy subcutaneous fat that accumulates under our skin, and the visceral fat that girds our bellies and surrounds our vital organs, are instead manufactured within our bodies from the sugars and starches that we consume, and not from the animal, vegetable, or dairy fats.[83]

Some research suggests that the cholesterol in foods such as eggs is chemically and physically different from the cholesterol in our blood. A key element is the size of cholesterol molecules. Many doctors are now less concerned with cholesterol rates and are paying more attention to the ratios between three types of cholesterol in blood: high-density lipoprotein (HDL), low-density lipoprotein (LDL), and triglycerides.[84]

The natural fats found in eggs, uncured bacon, grass-fed beef, fatty fish such as salmon and bluefish, nuts, milk, cream, butter, and beans are important components of healthy eating. Evidence is building that these natural fats tend to satisfy our appetites so that we eat less food overall. Dieters might find the secret to weight loss by eating more natural fats and eating less salt, sugar, and other sweeteners, all of which increase their appetites.

The natural fats also bolster our immune systems, preventing or delaying development of many diseases, including osteoporosis, eye cataracts and macular degeneration, as well as prostate cancer and some other forms of malignancy. It has also been shown that natural fats in our diets help to metabolize cholesterol, calcium, and vitamin D, all of which have beneficial effects.[85]

Once again, we may be saved by a universal intelligence that has already made adjustments to the metabolic code within some of our children that might compensate for future shortages of food. Many parents of Crystal Children have noted that their offspring eat far less food than their parents and older siblings. It is not unusual for these children to maintain healthy weights while eating only one meal a day. They also tend to enjoy fresh vegetables like asparagus, spinach, beets, and broccoli that children in the past have often refused to eat.

Health and Healing

While medical science has made enormous progress in the diagnosis and treatment of illnesses, the high cost of treatments and tests has made them less available to large segments of the population. At the same time, increasing administrative and insurance costs have resulted in an inability of general and family practice doctors to maintain their independence.

Medical practitioners and politicians alike now recognize that the current system is not sustainable and that costs are continuing to rise out of proportion to the rest of the economy. We do not yet have agreement on any workable solutions to these problems, but the shift we are now experiencing may offer some relief through changes in our attitudes toward illness and health, as well as increasing recognition of our own innate abilities to heal ourselves.

We have become so engrossed with our diseases, medications, and treatments that they have become the basis for personal identity for many people. Listen to the talk in any doctor's waiting room, or go to any gathering of elderly persons, and you will hear conversations dominated by descriptions of illnesses, operations, and treatments.

Comparing the numbers and costs of medicines seems to have become a game of who has the most for some people. We take medications to treat diseases that we have, to prevent diseases we do not have, and to counter the side effects of other medications and treatments.

Until the middle of the twentieth century, health care meant treatment of illness, with little attention given to preventive measures. For centuries before that, medicine had traditionally been considered to be more art than science, as early doctors actually knew very little about the nature of disease and illness. Yet the earliest practitioners were often able to cure their patients' problems through the use of incantations, herbal remedies, and ancient rituals. These cures worked primarily because the patients believed that they would.

As scientific experimentation developed, physical causes of disease such as viruses, bacteria, and genetic mutations were identified. Chemical drugs and physical operations were developed to treat the symptoms and to eradicate the root physical causes of illness. Surgeons learned to wash up before operating. When doctors became scientists, though, they seem to have lost the ability to also be artists.

Some pioneers in medical research are beginning to realize that our bodies hold a remarkable and underused ability to heal themselves. They call it psychoneuroimmunology.[86] We have not used this ability largely because we do not realize we have it. We have been indoctrinated by pharmaceuticals producers and hospital corporations to believe that only drugs or operations can cure us.

Leaders in the medical community are beginning to realize that many illnesses, diseases, and even accidents are a response to some form of psychological need. By identifying these psychological needs and treating or accepting their root causes, doctors of the future may be able to guide their patients to recovery or at least to acceptance of the experience of illness.

These ideas may seem strange to most readers, as they conflict with everything we have been taught about health, illness, and medical treatment. Let's take a closer look before we discard them, though, as they hold a potential key to the solution of our current health-care dilemma.

First, divide disease into two basic categories: illnesses that develop in otherwise healthy individuals and illnesses we bring with us when we are born. The latter group includes debilitating diseases that arise before a person reaches adulthood.

Now, for the purposes of thinking this through, consider what psychological factors might lay at the root of any disease. Stress would surely top this list. Stress reduces our immune responses, making us more susceptible to common colds, influenza, headaches, backaches, and muscle strains. Extreme stress can lead to heart attacks, strokes, and accidental injuries.

Severe handicaps change the world for those who develop them. Such conditions might be a result of needing to escape unbearable life situations, from an overwhelming need for attention, or from a desire at some unknown psychological level to experience life in this way.

This desire for a particular life experience can also help us to understand why some people come into this world with severe illnesses or handicaps from birth or develop such conditions in childhood. Perhaps this challenge is part of their life plan that was chosen before birth.

A related reason that is found with high consistency in spiritual texts, including Seth, Michael, and Kryon, is the idea that a child might come into this world with a severe or fatal medical condition for the sole purpose of enabling its parents to experience a particular life lesson.

We read every day of people who have succumbed to a serious illness after "a courageous battle." This may sound like a semantic argument, but taking the attitude that you are in a battle for survival immediately puts you in a position of accepting that you might lose the fight. Even if you survive, you will suffer irreparable damage to your body and psyche.

Instead of declaring war on your illness, you need to acknowledge it. Then get to work figuring out why you allowed it in to begin with. Fix the problems in your life that led to the disease and you improve your odds of recovery and survival.

Exploration of our self-healing abilities is an area that promises huge returns on relatively small investments. The use of meditation, visualization, and more healthy living habits all hold promise. While we should continue to rely on the knowledge and skills of our medical professionals, as well as the tests and treatments that are now available to us, we can use our innate self-healing abilities to assist those traditional treatments in order to more rapidly recover from our illnesses.

There are many among us who are able to take this exercise a step further and make it work on others. These natural healers may not be credentialed doctors or scientists; they are our friends, neighbors, and family members who have a special ability. They can actually bring healing energy to others by touch or by will. These healers are the new artists of medicine, and we should expect them to become more common in this new age.

What we need to do is expand the way we deal with disease by including nonchemical and nonphysical treatments in our curative processes. We need to realize that illness comes from within and not from outside forces. While we recognize that certain environmental forces can trigger disease, we must also see that those forces do not affect everyone they touch, but only act as catalysts for illness in those who have some sort of inner need to be sick.

In sum, one solution to our health-care problems involves a few simple steps: stop celebrating illness, identify its root cause, decide to be well, heal yourself, and maybe even develop the ability to heal others. This is not to infer that we do not need hospitals, medicines, and skilled physicians to cure our illnesses. Many of us would not be alive today without them.

Religion and Spirituality

Under the new world energy, spirituality is likely to flourish while traditional religious structures and organizations struggle and eventually fade away or morph into new roles. Individuals no longer need agents such as priests, rabbis, imams, or other intermediaries to communicate with their higher powers.

Churches may survive long after religions have died, serving as centers of social and cultural activities. Some of the more enlightened religious followers, such as the Unitarian/Universalists, Buddhists, and Quakers might adapt to the new reality. Spiritualist churches could thrive.

Religious mythology and ritual will probably endure, as they are important aspects of our culture and serve crucial psychological needs. The fraudulence of false dogma and altered texts that have been added by men over the centuries will no longer be acceptable to an enlightened populace, however. Clerics will need to stop preaching fear and start teaching enlightenment.

We might also expect the argument between evolution and creationism to eventually determine that both sides are partly right and partly wrong. The key to the solution of this conundrum may be recognition of the concept of intelligent design, although not in the form currently defined by the Christian fundamentalists.

The idea that the earth was created in seven days only a few thousand years ago clearly falls into the realm of mythology. On the other hand, Charles

Darwin's concept that species evolve through survival of the fittest may also be incomplete.

As scientists open their minds to broader thinking, they might come to realize that the earth and all its inhabitants were spontaneously created over time by a superior energy force. They might discover that our planet has evolved, and every species evolves, not only through survival of the fittest, but also through a process that we might call the introduction of new models.

We are routinely surprised by the discovery of plant and animal species alive today that were long thought to be extinct. We may be even more surprised in the future to discover entirely new varieties of plants and animals—possibly including human beings—that are genetically different enough to be considered new forms of the species. It could be that, just as we constantly improve and upgrade our vehicles, appliances, and other material goods, so too does God constantly improve and upgrade His products on earth.

Changing Relationships

The institution of marriage is now being tested as never before and appears to be evolving into something very different from its traditional definition. The Bible of Western religions speaks often of men taking wives but does not mention marriage. When these scriptures were written, taking a wife meant having intimate relations and siring children. The culture of the time required that the man support his wife for the rest of his or her life. It did not, however, limit a man to one wife, and men and their wives did not necessarily live together in family units.

When the culture became more complex and the rule of civil law developed, marriage contracts began to evolve that bound couples to monogamous unions primarily to protect the woman's ability to survive in a male-dominated society. Marriage ceremonies and rituals were not common at first, but simple declarations of marriage—often unilateral—were all that was required. In some places even today, such common-law marriages are still considered legal and binding.

Society is beginning to realize that marriage as we have known it no longer fits the way we now live. Fewer than half of all marriages endure, and divorce—which has often been used to publicly punish private behavior—has become a common procedure that often involves little more than a few minutes in court.

Marriage has effectively been redefined in recent years, but we have yet to publicly acknowledge the change. Two issues are now forcing our society to face the need to change how we deal with both the legality and morality of marriage: one is the question of nontraditional unions between same gender couples; the other is the emerging parity of women with men in all aspects of our lives.

One likely outcome of the current debate is a separation of the legal contract from the emotional ritual. We might maintain the ritual, either religious or civil, as a means of personal emotional commitment between two self-sufficient individuals, while setting up a separate legal process to protect the interests of both parties if and when the emotional commitment fades.

Many people, especially those entering a second or third marriage later in life, now sign prenuptial agreements or contracts. This practice might become universal even for first marriages in the near future. Protection of the rights and interests of children should remain paramount, but protection of established living standards of the parents might no longer be considered important.

As women become more financially and socially independent, as well as more fully integrated into businesses, governments, churches, and other institutions, the need for a legal marriage to protect their welfare becomes increasingly archaic and unnecessary.

Separation of the legal and emotional, or ritualistic, components of marriage could lead to a natural solution of the problem now being debated as to how to handle marriages between persons of the same gender. With a clearer distinction between legal obligations and moral purposes, there might be less confusion of the issue by religious dogmatists and conservative politicians.

Life and Death

A related benefit to better healing will be dramatic changes in life expectancy. Have you noticed how many people seem to be dying at younger ages, while others continue to live vibrant and active lives well into their eighth decade or more? As we move into the new earth conditions, expect to see those who cannot or will not become enlightened and adjust to the energy and cultural changes leave us at younger ages.

At the other end, expect to see those who do become more enlightened and adapt to the new energy living much longer. Our bodies were designed to last forever and have the ability to constantly regenerate at the cellular level. As we age, however, our glands reduce production of hormones that enable this cellular regeneration.[87] Evidence is beginning to emerge that we can slow—or even reverse—this process through changes in diet, exercise, intent, and expectations.

Demographers who are now predicting world food shortages from growing populations and longer life spans need not worry, though. As our lives lengthen, we will need to return fewer times before achieving full enlightenment. The combination of fewer new births and the early deaths of those who do not adapt is likely to result in a net reduction in total world population from what it is today.

Seth says we choose how and when to die, and that we move on when the conditions of this world are no longer fitting or comfortable to us. Death is unavoidable, and yet we have been taught to fear it at all costs. We spend fortunes extending lives past the point where they have any meaning or purpose, suffering painful months or years of unrewarding existence on chemical drugs that only postpone the work of our fatal diseases.

What is this fear that compels us to hold on to a life that is no longer worth living? Rationalists, who cannot conceive of an immortal existence and who believe that our lives are simply a random experience that ends with death, might be reluctant to let go. Those who have been taught that leading an imperfect life condemns them to eternity in hell might try to postpone the inevitable.

When we begin to understand that physical death in this reality does not extinguish the person within, and that there is no punishment in the afterlife for behavior in this one, we might no longer fear it. We would, of course, continue to mourn for those who move on, but we would grieve only for the loss of their presence in our own lives.

Funerals are a ritual the living use to adjust to the passing of people who were close to us. We look at the embalmed body and realize that the person we knew no longer inhabits it. We soften our loss by sharing our grief with family and friends. Funerals honor the dead but serve the living. We mourn not for the deceased but for ourselves.

For most of us, funerals are sad and depressing. We speak in hushed voices, listen to lugubrious music, read bible passages taken out of context, and wonder how we can ever carry on. Why do we behave in such a depressing manner? We may be reluctant to show anything but grief out of respect for family members. Beneath the surface, though, we may behave this way as a reaction to our inner fears.

The death of another person forces us to confront our own mortality. It stirs the fears of hell and damnation that our religious leaders have preached at us. It makes us realize that we all face something that we know nothing about. It is change, and change is frightening to most of us.

As we become more enlightened, these attitudes should change. Funerals could become celebrations of a life well lived, much as they traditionally have been practiced in Ireland and New Orleans. We would still mourn for ourselves but share stories that celebrate the life of the one who has passed, realizing that when this life on earth is done, new adventures await in the world of spirit.

Rise of the Unknown

Our current mythology assumes there are advanced societies living on other planets similar to our earth. There are about 200 billion sun-like stars in our galaxy and, according to astronomers, many billions of planets that could be like the earth.[88] The concept of traveling through space to other planets and other galaxies has appeared in our thoughts and literature for several centuries.

For the past fifty years we have been sending people into space to explore our earth and its moon. We have sent unmanned satellites to Mars and on flights that passed close to other planets. This exploration has often produced more questions than answers, however, and has led the more advanced physicists to question many of our basic scientific assumptions.

It is likely that the future will bring us into contact with beings from other worlds. We do not yet know whether this contact would be physical or through communications of some nature. Kryon tells us, for instance, that some—but not all—crop circles are actually cryptic messages from extraterrestrial beings. He says the others are fakes that were created by earthly pranksters.[89]

It is not likely, though, that we will be able to physically transport our bodies very far beyond our own planet without dire consequences. What our scientists have not yet recognized is the fundamental organic connection between our physical bodies and our planet. There are reasons why outer space, the moon, and even the polar regions of the earth are such brutally hostile environments for human beings. As we learn more about the earth's magnetic forces and the energy connections between our bodies and our planet, we might come to better understand these reasons.

A Different Kind of Reality

Our world has changed, but the changes we have seen so far are only a hint of what we might see over the next few decades. We have been living in a world of three physical dimensions plus time as a fourth dimension. Kryon says that we are now adding a fifth dimension where we incorporate into our daily lives the knowledge, wisdom, and abilities of our higher spiritual selves.[90]

The veil between our earthly existence and the realm of angels and spirits that we have worshiped and honored—but could not prove to exist—is disappearing. As a result, each of us might eventually become aware that we are angels living an earthly experience. We might see that there is a greater part of ourselves on the other side of the veil. We could recognize some close friends in the spirit world that are watching over us, helping us make decisions, guiding our thoughts and actions, and sometimes protecting us from our own stupidity.

As we gain spiritual awareness and become more enlightened, we should begin to act in a more spiritual, angelic, and godly manner, and learn to bring miracles into our own lives. We could also gain far more control over our lives and the events in them than we ever dreamed might be possible.

PART V – WHAT THIS MEANS TO US

<u>The Energy of Thought</u>

Before we move on to suggestions of how we can each adjust to the new world conditions, let's review the basic nature of our world and our universe. Albert Einstein taught us that the universe is made up of pure energy. He showed that all matter is simply energy moving at different frequencies and that energy is never spent nor lost, only changed into another form or place.

More recently, specialists in quantum physics have begun to realize that our thoughts are a form of energy and that thoughts can actually change the behavior of matter at the molecular level. They have also found that our thoughts may differ from other forms of energy in that they can apparently travel long distances without losing power, and at speeds many times faster than the speed of light, which limits the velocity of all other known forms of energy.[91]

It logically follows that, if our thoughts influence the behavior of atoms, and since all matter is composed of atoms, our thoughts should be able to influence the behavior of all matter. As this line of inquiry is explored further, research might find that all of this universal energy, from that of the cosmos to that of our individual cells and DNA, can be influenced in ways that we have not before imagined, by our own thoughts and by planetary and celestial actions.

There is growing evidence that each of us has an innate ability to manipulate our physical reality through our expectations, intent, and desires. Could it be that our universe is simply a thought, or an infinite collection of thoughts? Might we each be only an idea living in an imagined reality? The evidence, both spiritual and scientific, is pointing us in that direction.

If it is true that all things—every subatomic particle in our reality—is only a thought, and if it is true that thoughts can travel unlimited distances at nearly instantaneous speeds, then we may have found an explanation for how our essence—our souls—exist both within and separate from our physical bodies.

That might help to explain how we arrived on this planet from wherever we originated, how we maintain some form of consciousness after leaving our physical form, and how we go somewhere else when our bodies die. It might also be a clue to how we might be able to travel to other planets or galaxies despite the magnetic connections of our bodies to this planet.

Instead of encasing astronauts in dangerous simulations of earth environments such as rocket ships, space stations, and lunar colonies, maybe scientists should examine the possibility of placing their bodies into states of suspended animation while their energy entities explore our universe. And, taking this concept another step, could it be that our planet has been infiltrated by aliens from other worlds that have already perfected this technique? We might be under close observation and not even know it.

The Scriptures tell us that Jesus Christ could walk on water, turn water into wine, and raise the dead, then suggest that anything he could do we can do, and that, with faith in Him, we can do even greater things.[92] Two thousand years later we still have not mastered any of these things. There is growing evidence, though, that manipulation of our physical environment, both individually and in groups, is not only possible but more common than we know.

Religious believers know the power of prayer to bring healing to the sick and relief to the suffering. Large groups sharing common thoughts might be able to alter the weather, calming stormy seas or bringing rain to parched crops. Many of us have already learned how to manifest small miracles in our lives. Kryon tells us that this ability has become far easier under the new earth energy. Why aren't we doing it more?

New inventions, scientific breakthroughs, music, and other creative ideas often come to us while we sleep. Thomas Edison worked long hours but kept a cot in his laboratory where he would often nap for a few hours before awakening with the answers to problems he was facing. Mozart said his music, even the symphonies, came to him as finished works—all he did was write them down. Kryon says that every important scientific discovery was delivered from the spirit world in this way. We may find in the near future that we can bring into our lives anything we desire by simply stating our intent, thinking the thought, and letting it be.

The New Personal Reality

As the veil that has separated our earthly existence from our spiritual origins begins to lift, many people are discovering new abilities that they did not know they had. They are setting aside their fears and connecting with others in new and exciting ways. They are finding that their desires are becoming less self-centered and easier to bring into reality. They are becoming more intuitive and sensitive to the needs of others. They are learning how to heal themselves and others around them. They now have more direct contact with their spirit guides and their higher selves. They are, in effect, becoming godlier as they evolve more quickly than ever toward a state of true enlightenment.

Our planet is also changing. As its inhabitants have become increasingly enlightened, the energy of the earth has also changed to support and encourage the more advanced thinking and behavior of its people. The changes in the earth's magnetic grid that enable the more enlightened thinking and behavior have unfortunately also created massive disruptions, both physical and social.

The physical disruptions include climate change, with its consequent earthquakes, tornadoes, and other natural disasters. The social changes include shifting attitudes toward government, religion, and other basic institutions. The planetary changes are beyond our control, but we do have some power to deal with the social changes at an individual and personal level.

Seth, Kryon, and *A Course in Miracles* all tell us that Human beings are motivated by two basic emotions: one is love; the other is fear, which is the opposite of love. All other emotions arise from either love or fear. Hatred and bigotry are fear-based; compassion and generosity are love-based. War and conflict arise from fear; peace and fulfillment come from love. For the past two millennia, our societies, and our personal interactions, have been driven primarily by fear.

This paradigm is now changing. As we move to the next level of global consciousness, more of our thoughts and actions will be driven by love and compassion. This change could eventually lead to the complete elimination of poverty, crime, war, unfair competition, avarice, and greed. Sociologists already know that problems such as substance abuse, domestic violence, street gangs, and infant mortality are far more prevalent among people who are suffering extreme poverty and lack of hope.

The most important effect of this change is likely to be the growth of trust. It will begin as each of us learns to trust ourselves and our own judgments. We might then begin to trust those with whom we live, work, and interact on a daily basis. Someday we may come to trust strangers and maybe even our governments. Most importantly, we could set aside our ultimate fears and trust our God.

Fear has been the primary tool used by governments of all kinds and at all levels to keep the masses in line. In totalitarian societies, it is fear of death or imprisonment and torture; in free societies, it is fear of other governments, political opponents, and most recently, terrorists.

Fear has also been used by nearly all of the world's religions to control their adherents' thoughts and behavior. Foremost of these has been the fear of a wrathful and judgmental god. Church leaders have created myths surrounding the concepts of heaven and hell, devils and demons, sins and holy laws, that have no purpose other than to frighten their congregants into obedience to their will.

Our world is entering an age where true world peace is not only possible, but also essential to our survival. We are seeing class and ethnic definitions disappear, and we are beginning to realize that we are all of the same origin, with no fundamental differences between what we have mislabeled as races, clans, castes, or tribes. We may be a diverse bunch, but we all share a single planet.

Once we have joined hands as earthlings, we will be better prepared to make contact with beings from other worlds that some people believe have been watching us for a long time. If this is true, international relations are likely to seem like child's play compared to intergalactic relations. As Ronald Reagan reportedly commented to Mikhail Gorbachev, during their first summit meeting in Geneva, an alien invasion would make the differences between our countries seem trivial.[93]

What You Can Do

We are beginning to see what's happening in our world. It should be evident that the changes we are seeing in our planet, our weather, our society, our governments, our churches, and ourselves are part of a fundamental shift unlike anything we have seen before. It should also be apparent that there is very little, if anything, that any of us can do, either individually or collectively, to reverse or stop these changes. Our material assets are being drained away by the collapse of the world economy or are being destroyed by storms and other natural calamities. The businesses that employed us, sustained us, insured us, and served us, are folding or severely contracting.

As a result, we are no longer able to live as well as our parents did, and younger adults struggle to survive economically even with good educations and strong work habits. Retirement has become a distant dream for many, seemingly available now only to the wealthiest people. The religious institutions that we have traditionally turned to for emotional support during hard times increasingly seem to be out of touch with reality.

The one thing we can do is change ourselves. We can change the way we think and the way we live. The shift in earthly energy that is making it harder to live as our parents did is also making it easier for each of us to control our individual thoughts and actions. At the same time, we are being forced to take more personal responsibility for the effects of those thoughts and actions.

The rules have changed. We are being freed from control by our governments, our churches, and other people. It is becoming easier to live from the inner knowledge of who we are and to recognize what our individual purpose is supposed to be for our lifetimes on this earth.

So how are we supposed to think and act in order to adjust to this new energy? Here is a simple two-part test: whenever you are confronted with a new idea, or something happens that forces you to change your behavior, think about how you react to the change. Under the old negative energy, you would act out of fear and apprehension. You might become angry, defensive, and frustrated, and that anger might turn into illness, depression, violence, or other inappropriate behavior.

Now imagine how you might react under the new positive energy. You could look for ways that the change could benefit you or improve the world situation. You would adjust to it, and move on. Then imagine how quickly and how deeply our world would change if everyone thought this way. The most enlightened among us would simply accept change as normal and not react to it at all.

WHAT'S HAPPENING

If you are accustomed to praying, continue doing it, but think about what you are praying for. Prayers that convey love and compassion for others are far more effective than requests for personal favors or retribution. Most of us were taught as children how to pray. We pray for forgiveness, protection, or the realization of our dreams. Some of us were also taught to give thanks for what we have, regardless of how meager it might be. But were you ever taught to listen to God?

We know how to talk to God, but few of us know how to listen to Him. Perhaps we are turned off by the inanity of political leaders who tell us that God told them to wage war, or by the insanity of psychotics who claim God told them to murder their neighbors. Yet we all constantly receive advice and guidance from the spirit world.

These messages arrive while we are sleeping in the form of dreams, and while we are awake as intuition and gut feelings. Now that the barrier between the material world and the spirit world is beginning to lift, we can more easily get direct answers to specific questions. One good way to do this is through the ancient practice of meditation.

Meditation is simply a technique for quieting your mind in order to let inner knowledge and messages from the spirit world come through to you. It does not require specialized training, mystical mantras, or any psychic abilities. You do not need a shrine or special place to practice it. It can work as well on a crowded subway as in a peaceful meadow, although it is much easier—especially for beginners—to meditate in a quiet environment.

The secret of successful meditation is to clear your mind of all distractions and conscious thoughts. At first, try to find a quiet place to sit. If possible, face the earth's equator in order to better align your body with the planet's magnetic grid. Concentrate on relaxing your body, beginning at the top of your head, and following every muscle to the tip of your toes.

Focus on your breathing. Feel your lungs filling with air then exhaling. Imagine the earth's magnetic energy coming up through the soles of your feet, coursing through your body, and then exiting through the crown of your head.

Block out any distracting sounds or visions. Discard or reject any conscious thoughts that try to intrude on your feelings of quiet, gratitude, and peace. Ignore outside sounds and other stimuli. Clear your mind of as much intrusive thought as you can. Set aside thoughts of chores that need to be done and other worries. Suspend the arrogance of your ego, and feel the reality of your soul. Take whatever time you need to feel completely free and relaxed for the moment.

When you have cleared your mind of thoughts and distractions, listen for the messages. They do not usually come as voices. They may not come to you as coherent thoughts. More likely, you will sense feelings that lead you to know what you need to do to solve your problems and overcome obstacles that stand in the way of reaching your dreams.

Do not dwell on these feelings or think about them now. When you sense that you have heard the messages, write out your thoughts or the feelings that you sensed during your meditation. Now act on those thoughts and feelings. Try to meditate at least once a day. Meditations done immediately before sleeping can lead to deeper sleep and the answers to your questions coming to you in your dreams. With practice, you might learn to meditate several times a day, no matter where you are or what might be going on around you.

Meditation is also a powerful technique for self-healing. Here are two simple exercises that illustrate the possibilities inherent in this line of thinking. While you are reading this, raise your right hand. Now think about how you did this. Raising that hand required accurate coordination of hundreds of muscles and nerves. Did you consciously think about which muscles and nerves to use? Of course not. You simply decided to raise your hand,

and your body's natural resources made all the detailed decisions that allowed it to happen.

To tap into your body's natural healing ability, start with the same action: simply decide to do it. The next time you develop some sort of ache or pain, or any other early symptom of illness that you would rather not endure, see your doctor, take your medicines, and then simply decide to be well. You will be astounded at how well this works.

If you have been suffering from a persistent or chronic condition such as back pain, headache, skin irritation, or other malady, try adding meditative visualization to help your doctor heal you. This technique also works for serious conditions such as tumors and neurological diseases.

First, go into your normal meditative state. Now visualize the condition you want to cure. Put yourself inside your body. Look at the bones and muscles that are affected. If necessary, move on to the cellular level and visualize the affected cells. You do not need to have any anatomical knowledge of what these body parts actually look like. Just imagine what you think they might be and how the diseased condition looks.

Now visualize that diseased condition turning into a healthy condition. See that deformed tissue or odd cell turning normal. Watch that strained muscle or torn nerve heal itself. Now just let it go. That's right—stop thinking about it. Go back to what you were doing. Within a few days, you should see dramatic improvement. Enjoy the amazed look on your doctor's face when you have your next checkup and the symptoms that were troubling you have disappeared.

This practice is also effective for preventing disease and maintaining good health. Each day, when you meditate, focus on a single organ or area of your body and visualize it strong and healthy. In doing this, you not only state your intent but also build awareness of your physical conditions and bring them into balance with your spiritual and mental being. This is the secret to health and longevity.

Create the Life You Want

The magnetic energy of our planet has changed in a way that makes it much easier for all of us to work closely with the spirit world to co-create the lives we desire. Why should we try to go so far as to change our personal visions of the world? The answer is two-fold: first, because the old ways are no longer working under the new earth energy; and second, because we are now developing the ability to create for ourselves much more rewarding and productive lives. Now let's see how we can ratchet this thinking up a few notches.

Seth introduced us to the nature of personal reality a generation ago. He said our thoughts create our reality. In other words, our world becomes what we individually and collectively expect it to be. To change our reality we need only to change our thoughts and expectations.

This is not a new idea. The Reverend Norman Vincent Peale preached and wrote of the power of positive thinking more than half a century ago. Motivational speaker and writer Earl Nightingale called this concept *The Strangest Secret* on a recording he produced at about the same time.

Millions of people heeded the words of these men and changed their lives by changing their thinking. We could do it then; we can do it faster and easier now. Dreams and desires that once took months or years to bring to fruition, can now become real in weeks or days. Future generations may be able to bring thoughts to reality instantaneously.

Remember that everything in our universe is simply energy in various forms. That includes all forms of matter, all living organisms, and all of our thoughts. Know that every bit of this energy can be changed by our own conscious thoughts. Our four-dimensional world is only a small portion of reality.

Cosmologists have identified eleven dimensions of energy in all atoms; Kryon tells us they are missing one, but that we are not yet ready to know what that dimension is.

He also says that our DNA has twelve dimensions, including one of magnetic energy that encodes the conditions that existed at the moment of our birth. This dimension is the one that allows astrological influences to affect our thinking and behavior.

Kryon says that we can change our DNA through conscious thought and statement of intent. We are no longer limited in any way by our physical being or our physical environment. We just have not yet learned how to overcome these obstacles solely by changing our thinking and our intent.[94]

If you remain skeptical, here are a couple of simple exercises you can do to demonstrate your own power to better control and create your reality. The easiest of these was suggested by Seth. When you go to bed tonight, tell yourself to wake up at a certain time. This might be in the middle of the night, at your usual time, or some time later. You will awaken at that time.

Another exercise suggested by Seth and also described by Kryon, is creating parking spaces when and where you need them. To do this, picture the space you want opening up just when you need it.

Then know and expect that it will—this will not work if you hold any shred of doubt. Kryon calls this the phenomenon of the parking angel. It involves your higher self or spirit guides—your parking angels—coordinating your needs with the needs of another person who decides to vacate the space you want at the precise time that you want it. As strange as it sounds, this works.

While these may seem to be trivial exercises, they demonstrate how deeply and pervasive our spirit guides are involved in our daily lives. Mine seem to enjoy crossword puzzles as much as I do, often giving me answers before I have read the clues.

When you get good at creating parking spaces, move on to changing red traffic lights to green as you approach them. When you see how this works, take it a step further, and start creating opportunities for yourself by thinking the thoughts and stating the intent at work, in your relationships with others, in your sports and games, in your financial dealings, and in whatever creative endeavors you enjoy. This is indeed the strangest secret, and it is your personal path to fulfillment.

The key to opening up these newfound abilities is learning to communicate and work with your spirit guides to make it happen. These guardian angels have no other purpose than to guide us, protect us from our own bad ideas and decisions, and to help us create our lives on this earth. These are the powers that open doors of opportunity and place roadblocks in the way when we start moving in the wrong direction. You might think of them as God's agents assigned only to you.

Signs of Enlightenment

If it is true that each of us is following a path toward enlightenment, and if it is true that the new planetary energy allows us to move much faster along that path than we could before now, then we ought to have some way to measure our progress. How are we to know if we are actually becoming more enlightened or simply learning new ways to navigate our route through a complex and chaotic world?

Michael's description of changes in thinking and behavior of the various soul ages might be a good place to start. We could also apply Doctor Menninger's criteria of emotional maturity, and look to Abraham Maslow's list of characteristics of self-actualizing personalities. The social and cultural changes described in Part II of this book offer another measure of progress that can be used to measure individual enlightenment.

The fearful, uncompassionate, and often violent behavior of Infant Souls obviously typify the least enlightened traits, so we could say that the reciprocal of these behaviors—trusting, compassionate, and peaceful—are measures of enlightenment. The rigid, controlling, and dogmatic traits of Baby Souls could also be seen as unenlightened. So more flexible, accepting, and freethinking traits would be more enlightened. Similarly, the egocentric, materialistic, and highly competitive natures of Young Souls could be measured against more caring, cooperative, and non-material attitudes of Mature and Old Souls.

The ability to feel true empathy and compassion for others, and to understand highly complex issues, are Mature and Old Soul traits that are not found in the younger soul ages. These could therefore be considered to be more enlightened. Mature and Old Souls also tend to be more creative, artistic, and individualistic than younger souls. They are less likely to participate in team activities and more likely to pursue solitary adventures in both work and play. These self-reliant traits would then seem to be more enlightened than the group activities of the younger souls.

Maslow reinforces these observations with his description of self-actualizing personalities. He says that self-actualizers have a more efficient perception of reality and more comfortable relations with it. He says they are more accepting of themselves, of others, and of nature. He finds them to be more problem-centered than ego-centered, and to display a sense of spontaneity, simplicity, and naturalness. All of these traits and behaviors could be defined as more enlightened.

Some of Maslow's descriptions of self-actualizers are remarkably similar to Michael's descriptions of Mature and Old Souls. He says they have a quality of detachment and a need for privacy. He describes their autonomy, independence, and resistance to enculturation or peer pressure. Maslow says that self-actualizers enjoy a continued freshness of appreciation. He found that they often have mystic moments and what he calls "peak experiences." He notes their creativity, philosophical thinking, and "unhostile sense of humor."

Maslow also describes the ability of self-actualizers to discriminate between means and ends, and between good and evil. Finally, he says that self-actualizers, despite their independent natures, hold to a democratic character structure and form deeper and more profound interpersonal relations.

Menninger's list of signs of emotional maturity includes the ability to deal constructively with reality, the capacity to adapt to change, and the capacity to find more satisfaction in giving than receiving. It speaks of attaining relative freedom from symptoms produced by tensions and anxieties.

Menninger describes the capacity to consistently relate to others with mutual satisfaction, and the ability to direct hostile impulses into constructive outlets.[95] These measures of emotional maturity could also be seen as measures of enlightenment, particularly his final one: the capacity to love.

Canadian research psychologist Robert Hare has devoted his career to the study of psychopathic behavior. Dr. Hare devised a psychological test that has become widely used by penal authorities to help determine which parolees are likely to resume psychopathic behavior if released from prison. In his book, *Without Conscience, The Disturbing World of the Psychopaths Among Us*, Dr. Hare lists a dozen key symptoms of psychopathic behavior.[96]

Dr. Hare says that psychopaths tend to be glib and superficial; egocentric and grandiose; and deceitful and manipulative. He adds that they have shallow emotions and lack empathy for others, or any feelings of remorse or guilt. While this description might seem like a universal fit for all politicians, note that Dr. Hare strongly advises that his test should only be applied by trained psychologists.

The characteristics identified by this test are remarkably similar to the characteristics of Infant Souls described by Michael. This does not imply that all Infant Souls are psychopaths, but it does add credence to the idea that the youngest souls are the least enlightened.

Dr. Hare also notes a connection between physical development of the human brain and the tendency for psychotic behavior. This connection may be the key to future scientific study of why certain people behave in anti-social ways while others of similar intelligence and background are model citizens.

The six major trends in worldwide thinking described in Part II of this book all fit this model of enlightened behavior described by both Michael and Maslow. The rise in personal independence results from the desire of more enlightened persons to work individually without interference from controlling bosses or other authority figures. The revelation of secrets and demand for integrity in all aspects of life arises from the ability of enlightened people to discriminate between good and evil. The move from competition to cooperation reflects the ability to form deeper interpersonal relations.

The balancing of masculine and feminine energy represents resistance to past cultural standards and the embracing of a more democratic character structure. A more efficient perception of reality would be a driving force behind a society motivated more by compassion than by fear. And finally, the fundamental change in attitudes currently occurring in our world demonstrates the effect of a population that has recently become far more enlightened by all of these standards than has ever been seen before.

How can you tell you are making progress on your journey toward enlightenment? Here is a short list of ways to measure yourself. There are many more, of course, but these will get you started. You might be tempted to try emulating these feelings, but that will not necessarily get you any further ahead. In describing how we create our own lives, both Seth and Kryon tell us that when you want to be a certain way, or try to be a certain way, that is what you get: a life of wanting or trying. When you simply know that you are this way, you will have achieved true enlightenment.

You take charge of your fears. While continuing to be cautious of everyday perils, you let go of your fear of people and events that are entirely beyond your control or that do not directly affect you. You learn to discriminate between imagined perils and real threats to your health, safety, or well-being. You recognize that bigotry, hatred, and mistrust are all reactions to unexpressed fears, and you eliminate these emotions from your thoughts.

You no longer let fear of failure—or fear of success—keep you from realizing your goals and dreams. You turn away from the fear-mongers that seem to dominate the news media and Internet.

You develop an ability to separate truth from fiction, and to know when truth has been unfairly distorted. You begin to trust others and, most important, you learn to trust yourself.

You stop worrying. You realize that the purpose of worry is to warn you of problems that need to be addressed. If they are within your power, you address those problems; if they are not, you let them go. Worrying about problems that are beyond your control has no purpose and only causes you needless stress and anxiety, which can lead to illness. You concentrate instead on the people, events, and conditions that you most want to have and enjoy in your life and you begin to attract those people, events, and conditions to you.

You rise above petty annoyances. You let the little annoyances of life pass without notice, so that they do not retard your real progress. You understand that the slowpoke in the car ahead of you that is making you late for your appointment may be keeping you from an unpleasant encounter with a dangerous driver ahead. You separate yourself from annoying people and situations. You focus on your long-term desires and are not tripped up by short-term snags.

You detach from results. You find that becoming emotionally attached to specific actions can sometimes lead you in the wrong direction. You see that not reaching some of your goals has sometimes saved you from unforeseen grief. You learn that accepting outcomes that differ from your visions can mean that you have been overruled by higher powers that know better than you. You begin to assume that everything happens for a reason, and that events may be neither as negative nor as positive as initial appearance might seem.

You move away from extremes. You have learned that life is far more complex than any of us can fully comprehend. You see that there are many shades of gray between the black and the white extremes of any problem, issue, or idea. You understand that every solution to any problem involves secondary reactions or side effects, and that those unintended consequences sometimes create new problems. Your ideas become less definitive and more nuanced. You realize that you do not always have to be right, or even to have a response to every issue.

You become accepting of others. You know that other people think and behave differently from you because they are uniquely themselves, just as you are. You do not judge others and are not affected by their judgments of you. You accept their ideas and behavior even when you completely disagree with them. You understand that we each define ourselves and are not defined by others. You begin to enjoy the differences between individuals.

You reset your moral compass. You realize that morality has little to do with church doctrine, political affiliation, sexual preference, or marital status. You accept that morality has everything to do with your own personal behavior, responsibility, and attitude toward others. You see that if someone else's behavior does not directly affect you, it is none of your business or concern. You set an example that pleases you, and you allow others to be free to follow their own course of conduct.

You forgive those who have hurt you. You stop dwelling on past injustices, as you realize doing so is holding you back from your goals. You find that forgiveness becomes a more natural reaction than blame in even the most aggravating situations. You may even reach the point where you thank those who have hurt you for the lessons that they taught you. In short, you no longer grant others permission to manipulate or abuse you.

You become more compassionate. You empathize with the feelings of others, and understand the reasons for their thinking, attitudes, and behavior. You realize that you can never fully understand another person, and you become more accepting of the role their lives play in your life. You understand that true compassion arises from deep within your heart and is far more than simple expressions of sorrow or caring.

You expect the best of everyone. You realize that every person is better than anybody else at being themselves. You know that nobody else can be better at being the person you are than you can. You let the inner person that is you shine, and you allow and encourage all the people around you to be themselves and to shine as you do. You see that life is not a zero-sum game in which one player has to lose for the other to win.

You become more generous. You freely give away your talents, abilities, friendship, support, and material things, having learned that everything you give away comes back to you many times over. You understand the abundance of the universe and know that you will always have what you need, although what you need might not always be what you think you want.

You overrule your ego. You find you no longer need to have the last word in a discussion or an argument. You know who you are and do not feel any need to impress others with your abilities, ideas, opinions, wisdom, or wit. You realize that nobody else's life is about you, and that you are more likely to succeed in your life by focusing on the needs and feelings of others.

You awaken to your purpose. You have identified the purpose for which you came into this world and live it every day. You have found the life of your dreams and been rewarded by the universe. You follow your heart and have become more self-sufficient. You no longer think of employment as working for somebody else, but use your natural talents and abilities to support yourself and your family doing what you most enjoy.

You consider what you can do as an individual to create income through service to others. You think "What can I do to improve the lives of other people?" not "What can I do to make money?" You know inside what you like and what you dislike. You listen patiently to the advice and counsel of others, but act on only what feels right for you.

You take charge of your life. You have turned your life in the direction you want it to go. You have found your spiritual center and become comfortable in it. You have become more independent. You do not let others manipulate or control you in any way. You take care of yourself. You take charge of your health and decide to be well. You identify and deal with any emotional issues or stresses that lead to illness. You practice meditation and self-healing techniques. You understand that health is normal and that all diseases and all accidents are signs of some imbalance in your life.

You become grateful. Whether you are meditating or not, you feel a sense of gratitude projecting from the center of your heart for the life you have, for your family, friends, talents, and everything else that is important to you. You express your gratitude often, through prayer and meditation, and through being openly thankful to everyone around you for everyday kindnesses. You constantly reflect those kindnesses back to others as another expression of gratitude.

You connect with your higher power. You know that some power greater than yourself influences every aspect of your life. Whatever you envision that power to be, whether it is saints, spirit guides, a higher self, Jesus, or God, you establish constant communication and work together with that higher power to create the life you desire.

You frequently experience what Abraham Maslow called peak experiences—moments of success beyond anything you ever imagined. You are no longer surprised by apparent miracles in your life. You come to fully expect that things will go your way and are always grateful when they do.

You feel serene. You are no longer stressed over daily existence. You have simplified your life so you have only those responsibilities that are important to you. You have reduced your schedule to a manageable level. You have learned how to gently say no to requests by others. You enjoy quiet times and do not need to have a television or music player always on. You are no longer distracted by your personal electronic devices.

You become loving. You have learned to love yourself and can therefore give unconditional love to others. You bring love and compassion to everything you do, everything you say, and everything you think. You realize that the source of real happiness does not lie in wealth and material goods, but in the quality of your relationships and the satisfaction you find in living and loving every day.

You become joyful. You experience frequent moments of unexplained happiness. You are more than happy, however. What you feel is pure joy. You love your life with all its complexity, challenge, disappointments, and rewards. You radiate an inner sense of joy that is apparent to everyone you encounter. You sometimes feel as if you will burst from the joy within you.

You are fulfilled. You feel that your life, despite its disappointments and flaws, is exactly as it should be. While you eagerly await the wonders of each new day, you desire nothing more in the way of material goods or social connections. You sense the appreciation and adoration of your family and friends, and have no desire to impress anybody else. You love the person that you are.

Isn't this the life you want—a life in which you feel joyful and fulfilled? This is where every one of us is headed. This is an enlightened life. We have, as a planet, reached a combined average level of enlightenment that allows us to move into a new planetary energy that will propel each of us along the path of enlightened growth much faster than ever before possible. Now it is up to each of us to use the new energy in pursuit of our dreams. In so doing, we will collectively create the world of peace, prosperity, and abundance that we all crave.

This is what's happening. We are now on the threshold of a completely new way of living in which we co-create our lives and our reality by working with our spiritual powers and using the talents and techniques that have not been easily available to us in the past.

Every one of us has been given a wonderful gift. The time has now come for each of us to open that gift and begin using it to create the lives that we desire. Set aside your fears, open your heart, and whatever you do, do it with integrity, compassion, and love. In doing this, we will collectively create the world that we all want—a world of peace, productivity and personal fulfillment.

EPILOGUE

A small ad in our regional newspaper caught my attention. There was to be a psychic fair held at the Wigwam, a Spiritualist retreat center in Onset, Massachusetts. The Village of Onset sits high on a bluff overlooking a beautiful inlet off Buzzards Bay at the western end of the Cape Cod Canal. It was originally established as a Spiritualist summer camp in 1877.

Onset's many little cottages on tiny lots started out as tent platforms for families who spent their summers there in the late 1800s. There is still a small independent Spiritualist congregation that meets in a house they call a church. Another group, which is affiliated with The National Spiritualist Association of Churches, holds services and classes during the warmer months in the Wigwam.

This unique building was constructed of wood in the shape of a Native American teepee in 1894. Its central supporting post was blessed by Native American shamans, who reputedly imbued it with healing energy. During the warmer months, the On-I-Set Wigwam Spiritualist Camp holds Sunday services and evening meetings there. I had been aware of this structure and its history, but had never attended any of its services or meetings.[97]

The psychic fair was disappointing. There were the expected readers of tarot cards, palms, and minds, along with a few people selling books and trinkets, and one with a Polaroid camera that supposedly photographed auras. I was not impressed. Nevertheless, I picked up a schedule of events and began attending services and meetings regularly.

I was intrigued by the apparent abilities of some of the leaders of these gatherings. These were, for the most part, not professionals but ordinary people who had developed abilities they claim are latent in all of us. Some were able to bring forth healing energy; others were able to bring forth messages from the spirit world.

Some of these mediums were better than others, but the best were simply astounding. I was soon convinced that this was no parlor game or sideshow activity, even when a spirit I recognized as being one of my great-grandfathers suggested I get a dog to keep me company.

At one of these meetings I met April Sheerin. April is a professional psychic who lives in New Hampshire and has taught courses in spirituality at the University of Massachusetts. April's ability to call forth messages from the spirit world is not as good as some of the other mediums I had seen at Onset. Her stories of contacts with angels sometimes stretch the limits of credulity. Her talent for getting inside the heads of individuals, however, and describing what might be motivating them to think and act as they do, is simply extraordinary.

April inspired me to write this book. In the course of a casual conversation, she asked what I did for a living. I told her I was mostly retired but still did some consulting in my career field of community planning. Then I said something that surprised me because I had not consciously thought about it. I said, "I don't want to do that anymore, but I don't have the resources to fully retire."

April asked what I would like to be doing, and I told her I like to write and have been told that I do it well. That evening, during a lecture in which April was encouraging her audience to follow their hearts, she looked me straight in the eye and said, "Write your book, and the income that you need will come to you."

Later, April told me that I would have five spirit guides helping me with my writing. She said I would be able to tell them apart because my handwriting would change depending on which guide was with me. I scoffed at this notion, partly because I write at a computer—not longhand—and partly because I had not at that time learned to work closely with spirit guides.

Now that the book is finished, however, I have changed my mind. Whenever I sat at the computer to write, the ideas and words would come through clearly, easily, and sometimes so fast I would have trouble keeping up on the keyboard. Often the sentence structure or word usage would be odd, which is unusual because I am a stickler for proper usage. That was what I was seeing instead of a handwriting change.

What really convinced me that I was receiving help from some unseen source, though, was what I call the "Wow moments". Nearly every day, as I reviewed what I wrote, I would think "Wow, I didn't know that." I was actually setting down thoughts and ideas that I had not consciously considered and that had not been triggered by my usual sources of information. On several occasions, I would read verification of some of these ideas in the course of my research days or weeks after writing them.

At no time did I go into a trance state, hear voices in my head, or feel that I was not in complete control of my writing. There is no question in my mind, though, that I was getting information from some unseen source. This is one of the latent abilities that we all brought with us when we were born but which we have not developed or used because our society has taught us that it is not possible.

My experiences at Onset reinforced many of the ideas and concepts that I had learned from reading Seth, Kryon, Walsch, *A Course in Miracles*, and the other works that I have cited here. They also led me to recognize the connection between these readings and the increasingly strange events that have been happening all over our planet.

Since that first day at the Wigwam, I have devoted most of my time and energy to further study of both the spiritual readings and current events. This book is the product of that study. I now understand that my personal purpose in this life is to share this knowledge with others. Never before have I been as energized and enthused by any project as I have by this one.

I hope you have enjoyed reading this book as much as I have enjoyed writing it. I have presented many ideas that fall far beyond the fringes of mainstream thinking, and have deliberately avoided strong arguments to bolster or defend those ideas. You are free to accept them or reject them. I encourage you to further explore the ideas I have outlined, though, and to welcome and celebrate the wonderful new world we are creating together.

Thank you for choosing this book,

Wesley Ewell

NOTES & REFERENCES

[1] The United States, Russia, Ireland, and Great Britain all have doomsday plans that outline actions to be taken in the event of nuclear holocaust. Great Britain's doomsday plan did not become known until June 2009. Other countries may also have similar plans.

[2] John Major Jenkins, *The 2012 Story: The Myths, Fallacies, and Truth Behind the Most Intriguing Date in History* (New York: Tarcher/Penguin, 2009) ISBN 978 1 58542 766 6.
Daniel Pinchbeck, *2012 The Return of Quetzalcoatl* (New York: Tarcher/Penguin, 2006) ISBN 1 58542 483 8.

[3] This subject is covered in detail in Lecture 8 of Professor Bart D. Ehrman's course, *The History of the Bible: The Making of the New Testament Canon*, published by The Teaching Company, 2005. More information is available on The Teaching Company website at www.teach12.com.

[4] The full text of Nostradamus' letter to his son can be found at www.crystalinks.com/nostradamus2.

[5] Thoreau wrote: "If a man does not keep pace with his companions, perhaps it is because he hears a different drummer. Let him step to the music he hears, however measured or far away." He never mentioned marching to a drumbeat, but has often been misquoted as such.

[6] Bronson Alcott's Fruitlands Farm has been restored and is now a museum in Hudson, Massachusetts. Its Web site is www.fruitlands.org.

[7] More information on Jane Roberts and Seth, as well as a source of CDs, books, videos, and conference schedules, can be found at: www.sethlearningcenter.org.

[8] Nicholas Campion, *The Dawn of Astrology* (London and New York: Continuum Books, 2008) ISBN: 978 1 84725 214 2. Professor Campion is head of the Sophia Centre for the Study of Cosmology in Culture and senior lecturer in archaeology and anthropology, University of Wales, Lampeter, where he is course director of the MA in cultural astronomy and astrology. He also teaches at Kepler College, Seattle.

[9] Ecclesiastes 3:1-8 (kjv). "For everything its season, and for every activity its time."

[10] Jose Stevens, Ph.D., Simon Warwick-Smith, *The Michael Handbook* (Sonoma, CA: Warwick Press, 1990). ISBN: 0 941109 00 3.

[11] John 3:3 (kjv), Jesus states "In truth, in very truth I tell you, unless a man has been born over again he cannot see the kingdom of God." This phrase is interpreted by some churches as needing to devote one's life to worship of Jesus. It could also be interpreted to mean reaching a level of enlightenment that allows one to see the world of spirit.

[12] This sentence is borrowed from the writings of Professor Emeritus Eugene Bammel and used with his permission.

[13] Brian Weiss, MD, *Many Lives, Many Masters* (New York: Fireside, 1988) ISBN: 978 0 671 65786 4.

[14] Spiritual author Robin Norwood, in her book *Why Me, Why This, Why Now*, (republished by Arrow Books, 2009) included a chart that suggested that souls mature emotionally over a series of lifetimes.

[15] Abraham Maslow, *Motivation and Personality* (New York: Harper, 1954. Second Ed., NY: Harper, 1970. Third Ed., NY: Addison-Wesley, 1987).

[16] Richard Lowry, ed., *Dominance, Self-Esteem, Self-Actualization: Germinal Papers of A. H. Maslow* (Monterey, CA: Brooks/Cole, 1973).

[17] Erik Erikson defined eight stages of psychosocial development within each person's lifetime. A concise summary of Erikson's stages can be found in an article by Arlene F. Harder at Learning Place Online: www.learningplaceonline.com/stages/organize/Erikson.

[18] Chelsea Quinn Yarbro, *Michael for the Millennium* (New York: Berkeley Books, 1995). Yarbro states that Ethiopia, Sudan, New Guinea, and Sri Lanka are countries where infant souls currently predominate, and that Borneo and Cambodia also have large populations of infant souls.

[19] *Anatomical Changes in the Emerging Adult Brain*, a study by Dartmouth College researchers Abigail Baird and Craig Bennett, appeared in the November 29, 2005 on-line issue of the *Journal Human Brain Mapping*.

[20] David R. Hubbard, MD, Managing Director of the Applied Functional MRI Institute in San Diego, California, has been exploring the connections between emotions and activity of various sections of the brain. The institute's website can be found at www.appliedfmri.org.

[21] Patricia S. Churchland, *Braintrust: What Neuroscience Tells Us about Morality* (Princeton, NJ: Princeton University Press, 2011) ISBN: 978 0 691 13703 2.

[22] This analysis was reported by biochemist Douglas C. Wallace in the March 1990 issue of *American Journal of Human Genetics*.

[23] Gregg Braden, "Choice Point 2012" essay in *The Mystery of 2012* (Boulder, CO: Sounds True, 2007).

[24] The full text of Van Auken's essay on the Aztec Sun Disk can be found at www.sleepingprophet.org/2012-Part1.

[25] Richard Tarnas, *Cosmos and Psyche* (New York: Penguin Group, 2007) ISBN: 978 0 452 28859 1.

[26] Specific information on sea level changes due to global climate change can be found at the U.S. Environmental Protection Agency website: www.epa.gov/climatechange/science/recentslc.

[27] Hurricane tracking diagrams and storm statistics by year can be found at the National Weather Service: www.nhc.noaa.gov/2010atlan.shtml.

[28] More details on tsunami occurrence can be found at NOAA Satellite and Information Service, National Geophysical Data Center, Tsunami Data and Information: www.ngdc.noaa.gov.

[29] A story reported by CNN.com March 20, 2002, quoted Larry Newitt of the Geological Survey of Canada saying "The magnetic pole, which has steadily drifted for decades, has picked up its pace in recent years and could exit Canadian territory as soon as 2004."

[30] More information on magnetic field reversals can be found at www.nrcan.gc.ca, a website of the Geological Survey of Canada.

[31] James Risen, "U.S. Identifies Vast Mineral Riches in Afghanistan," *The New York Times*, June 13, 2010.

[32] Barry A. Kosmin, Ariela Keysar, Principal Investigators, *American Religious Identification Survey 2008*. (Trinity College, 300 Summit Street, Hartford, Connecticut. www.americanreligionsurvey-aris.org). Professors Kosmin and Keysar are, respectively, director and associate director of Trinity's Institute for the Study of Secularism in Society and Culture.

[33] The full text of the publication can be found at the Pew Forum Web site: www.pewforum.org.

[34] See Martin Buber, *The Eclipse of God*; Emil Fackenheim, *What is Judaism?*, Pope John Paul II, *Faith and Reason;* or any of the works of Karl Barth or Alvin Plantinga. Special thanks to Professor Emeritus philosopher Eugene Bammel for the references and wording in this paragraph and his permission to use them.

[35] Abraham H. Maslow, Religions, Values, and Peak-Experiences (New York: Penguin, 1970). ISBN 0 1401 9487 8

[36] Ehrman, op. cit.

[37] ibid.

[38] Sig Synnestvedt, *The Essential Swedenborg* (West Chester PA: Swedenborg Foundation, 1977). ISBN: 0 87785 152 2

[39] ibid.

[40] Swedenborg's published works are available from The Swedenborgian Virtual Book Store, maintained by The

Swedenborgian Church of North America, www.swedenborg.org/bookstore/index.

[41] Swedenborg defined charitable as being compassionate toward others. His meaning is far broader than the current understanding of the word.

[42] Ralph Waldo Emerson, *Representative Men*, first published in 1850 and currently available for download through Google books.

[43] Mitch Horowitz, *Occult America* (New York: Bantam, 2009) ISBN: 978 1 61664 242 6.

[44] More information on Spiritualism and the Spiritualist Church can be found at the website of National Spiritualist Association of Churches at www.nsac.org.

[45] More information on Theosophy and The Theosophical Society of America, including a biography of Blavatsky, can be found on its website at www.theosophical.org.

[46] More information on Edgar Cayce and Association for Research and Enlightenment, Inc. can be found through the association's website: www.edgarcayce.org.

[47] This paragraph was paraphrased from the Noetics Institute history posted on its website, www.noetic.org. Dr. Mitchell's story is told in the book *The Way of the Explorer: An Apollo Astronaut's Journey Through the Material and Mystical Worlds*, available through the Institute.

[48] ibid.

[49] More information on the Institute of Noetic Sciences can be found on its Web site at www.noetic.org.

[50] Mitchell, op. cit.

[51] Helen Schucman and William Thetford, *A Course in Miracles* (The Foundation for Inner Peace: Mill Valley, CA, 1976.) ISBN: 0 9606388 8 1.

[52] The Foundation for Inner Peace, P.O. Box 598, Mill Valley, CA 94942. www.acim.org/index.

[53] One such organization is the Circle of Atonement, www.circleofa.org.
Another is the Community Miracles Center, www.miracles-course.org.

[54] Marilyn Ferguson, *The Aquarian Conspiracy* (J.P. Tarcher, Inc.: Los Angeles, 1980).

[55] More information about Neale Donald Walsch, his books, CDs, and conference schedule can be found on his Web site at www.nealedonaldwalsch.com.

[56] More information about Lee Carroll and Kryon can be found at www.kryon.com. The many citations of Kryon in this book are presented by permission granted during a face-to-face conversation between Lee Carroll and the author in Haverhill, Massachusetts, on August 13, 2011.

[57] Lee Carroll, *Kryon* (Book 1) *The End Times, New Information for Personal Peace* (The Kryon Writings: Del Mar, CA, 1993).

[58] Lee Carroll, *Kryon* (Book 7) *Letters From Home, Loving Messages From the Family* (The Kryon Writings, Inc.: Del Mar, CA, 1999) p.266.

[59] For a thorough explanation of the Harmonic Convergence, refer to the works of Jose Arguelles.

[60] Lee Carroll, *Kryon* (Book Eleven) *Lifting the Veil, The New Energy Apocalypse* (The Kryon Writings, Inc.: Del Mar, CA, 2007).

[61] Lee Carroll, *Kryon* (Book Ten) *A New Dispensation, Plain Talk for Confusing Times* (The Kryon Writings, Inc.: Del Mar, CA, 1993) p. 194.

[62] Ferguson, p. 15.

[63] Lee Carroll and Jan Tober, *The Indigo Children, The New Kids Have Arrived* (Hay House: Carlsbad, CA, 1999).

[64] A concise description of characteristics of Indigo Children can be found at the website of Wendy H. Chapman, who has recently published a book for parents called *The Complete Idiot's Guide to Indigo Children*. www.metagifted.org/topics/metagifted/indigo/indigoChildCharacteristics.

[65] Op. cit. *The Michael Handbook*, p. 53.

[66] For a more detailed analysis of Crystal Children, see Doreen Virtue, *The Crystal Children*, published by Hay House 2003. Dr. Virtue maintains a Web site at www.angeltherapy.com.

[67] While these characteristics of Crystal Children have been well documented in several books, this author has personally observed them in a young member of his own family.

[68] A good description and analysis of the DNA changes found in Crystal Children can be found in the book *The Children of Now* by Meg Blackburn Losey (New Page Books, 2007) ISBN: 978 1 56414 948 0.

[69] Martine Vallee, *Transition Now* (San Francisco: Red Wheel) p.240.

[70] *A Course in Miracles*, op. cit. *Manual for Teachers*, p.17.

[71] Reported by Bjoern H. Amland on Huffingtonpost.com June 6, 2011.

[72] For more information on the Milankovitch theory, refer to the website of the U.S. department of Commerce National Climatic Data Center at www.ncdc.noaa.gov/paleo/milankovitch.

[73] Kryon channeling observed by author August 13, 2011.

[74] Kryon channeling, January 16, 2011 in Boulder, Colorado, available on line at www.kryon.com/k_channel11_boulder.

[75] The change in West Point curriculum began with the partial replacement of military instructors with civilians. A comprehensive description of the effect of this change was described in a paper by Cpt. James P. Dyke, *Civilianization of the Faculty: A Change Whose Time Had Come* (West Point, 14 November 2001) available on the academy's website at www.usma.edu.

[76] *Michelle Flournoy Shaping Pentagon Policy*, Oxford Analytica (September 14, 2010) reported by Forbes.com.

[77] Experiments by French physicist Alain Aspect and collaborators first measured the speed of communication between subatomic

particles in 1980. Aspect's experiment was repeated by Swiss physicist Nicolas Gisin in 1997, as reported in Laszlo, op. cit.

[78] The concept of a vast number of parallel universes was first suggested by Hugh Everett, a doctoral candidate in quantum mechanics at Princeton University in 1957. Everett was so disheartened by the negative reaction of the scientific community to his theory that he left the field after earning his Ph.D. degree and became a government defense analyst. Several other cosmologists, including Stephen Hawking, have since built upon and refined Everett's theory. See also Michio Kaku, *Parallel Worlds, A Journey Through Creation, Higher Dimensions, and the Future of the Cosmos* (New York, Doubleday, 2005) ISBN: 0 7394 5658 X.

[79] Mitchell, op. cit.

[80] Carroll (Book 7) op. cit., p. 419.

[81] In Book 7, p. 334, Kryon speaks of the bio-deactivation of atomic waste as likely very soon, with harnessing of the magnetic grid being a future possibility.

[82] For a highly informative and readable treatise on this subject, see *Real Food, What to Eat and Why*, by Nina Planck (Bloomsbury 2006).

[83] Glen C, Griffin and William P. Catelli, *Good Fat, Bad Fat, Lower Your Cholesterol and Reduce Your Odds of Heart Attack* (Cambridge, MA, Perseus 1989, 1993, & 1997).

[84] Ibid.

[85] Ibid.

[86] More information on this subject can be obtained from the Psychoneuroimmunology Research Society, Inc., an international organization based in Pennsylvania whose stated purpose is to promote the study of interrelationships among behavioral, neural, endocrine, and immune processes and to encourage collaborations among immunologists, neuroscientists, clinicians, health psychologists and behavioral neuroscientists. Its website can be found at www.pnirs.org.

[87] Further information on cellular regeneration can be found at www.lef.org, the website of Life Extension Foundation.

[88] *The Occurrence and Mass Distribution of Close-in Super-Earths, Neptunes, and Jupiters.* Andrew W. Howard, Geoffrey W. Marcy, John Asher Johnson, Debra A. Fischer, Jason T. Wright, Howard Isaacson, Jeff A. Valenti, Jay Anderson, Doug N. C. Lin, and Shigeru Ida, *Science* 29 October 2010: pp. 653-655.

[89] Lee Carroll, *Kryon* (Book 3) *Alchemy of the Human Spirit, A Guide to Human Transition into the New Age* (The Kryon Writings, Inc.: Del Mar, CA, 1995) p.290; and *Kryon* (Book 6) *Partnering With God, Practical Information for the New Millennium* (The Kryon Writings, Inc.: Del Mar, CA, 1997) pp. 362-366.

[90] Carroll (Book Eleven) op. cit.

[91] For excellent descriptions of the characteristics of molecular energy, written in clearly readable form, see Ervin Laslo, *Science and the Akashic Field, An Integral Theory of Everything*, www.innertraditions.com.

[92] In John 14:12 (kjv) Jesus says "In truth, in very truth I tell you, he who has faith in me will do what I am doing; and he will do greater things still because I am going to the Father."

[93] A. Hovni, in an article entitled "The Shocking Truth, Ronald Reagan's Obsession With an Alien Invasion", published in the September 1988 Issue of *UFO Universe*, reported:
> The President first disclosed his recurrent thoughts about "an alien threat" during a December 4, 1985, speech at the Fallston High School in Maryland, where he spoke about his first summit with General Secretary Gorbachev in Geneva. According to a White House transcript, Reagan remarked that during his 5-hour private discussions with Gorbachev, he told [Gorbachev] to think, "How easy his task and mine might be in these meetings that we held if suddenly there was a threat to this world from some other species from another planet outside in the universe. We'd forget all the little local differences that we have between our countries ..."

[94] Lee Carroll, *Kryon* (Book Twelve) *The Twelve Layers of DNA, An Esoteric Study of the Mastery Within* (The Kryon Writings, Inc.: Del Mar, CA, 2010).

[95] The full list of Dr. Menninger's criteria for emotional maturity can be found on the Menninger Clinic's website at: www.menningerclinic.com/resources/emotional_maturity.

[96] Robert D. Hare, PhD, *Without Conscience, The Disturbing World of the Psychopaths Among Us* (New York, The Guilford Press 1993).

[97] A brief history of Onset village and the Onset Wigwam can be found at www.hollyhurstcottageinn.com/onsethistory. See also the website of the Wigwam at www.onisetwigwam.com.

www.ingramcontent.com/pod-product-compliance
Lightning Source LLC
Chambersburg PA
CBHW061635040426
42446CB00010B/1433